More Praise for Differentiate or Die

"Lucid, intelligent, and showing Trout's great knack for simplifying without oversimplifying."
　　　—Michael Bungey, Chairman and CEO, Bates Worldwide

"In the twenty-first century, successful companies must stand for something that sets them apart. Here is the prescription on how it's done, from two experts who've been through the competitive wars."
　　　—Lawrence Toal, Chairman and CEO, The Dime Savings Bank

Reach Jack Trout at www.troutandpartners.com

DIFFERENTIATE OR DIE

Survival in Our Era of Killer Competition

JACK TROUT

with

Steve Rivkin

JOHN WILEY & SONS, INC.

New York • Chichester • Weinheim • Brisbane • Singapore • Toronto

Published by John Wiley & Sons, Inc.
Published simultaneously in Canada.

This publication is designed to provide accurate and authoritative information in regard to the subject matter covered. It is sold with the understanding that the Publisher is not engaged in rendering professional services. If legal, accounting, medical, psychological, or any other expert assistance is required, the services of a competent professional person should be sought.

Library of Congress Cataloging-in-Publication Data

Trout, Jack.
    Differentiate or die : survival in our era of killer competition / Jack Trout, Steve Rivkin.
        p.   cm.
    Includes bibliographical references and index.
    ISBN 0-471-35764-2 (alk. paper)
    1. Marketing.   2. Advertising—Brand name products.   3. Brand name products.   4. Competition.   I. Rivkin, Steve, 1947–   II. Title.
    HF5415.T727 2000
    658.8—dc21   99-059991

Printed in the United States of America.

10 9 8 7 6 5 4 3

To Rosser Reeves,
the man who made the "unique selling proposition" famous.
He was truly a man ahead of his time.
Little did any of us realize just how competitive
the world would become.

PREFACE

For what seems like several lifetimes, my partners and I have been preaching the importance of being different.

In *Positioning* being different meant differentiating yourself in the mind of your prospect.

In *Marketing Warfare* being different meant using a differentiating idea to defend, attack, flank, or become a guerrilla.

In *The 22 Immutable Laws of Marketing* being different meant using a differentiating idea to build a brand.

In *The Power of Simplicity* being different meant using a strategy that was all about differentiation.

Being different is at the heart of everything we've done for almost thirty years.

You might assume that by now the message has been delivered. Everyone is busy building "differentiation" into their plans. And no one would leave home without his or her differentiating idea. Right?

Wrong.

What we tend to see are two types of organizations. One type still doesn't get it. They're out there doing battle with "higher quality" or "good value" or good old "better products." They feel that they are better than their competitors and that truth will out.

They surround themselves with gurus who talk about quality, empowerment, customer orientation, and various forms of leadership. Unfortunately, all of their competitors are surrounded by the same cast of "you can get better" gurus. Nothing different.

The other type of organization understands the need to be different. But after some prodding, they will admit that they just don't know how to do it. Their excuse: Our product or sales force just isn't that much different from our competitors'.

They tend to get sucked in by the motivation crowd that promises peak performance, a winning attitude, and effective habits. Unfortunately, the same cast of characters is hanging around and motivating their competitors. Nothing different.

And they don't get much help from the big-name academics. Harvard's Michael Porter, for example, does talk about the need for a unique position, but he never offers much help on how to be unique. Instead, he talks about strategic continuity, deepening strategic position, and minimizing trade-offs. And he talks to any competitor who will pay his fee. Nothing different.

And their advertising agencies aren't much better. They talk about bonding, likability, breakthroughs, and cool. To them it's all about being artful, not scientific. Nothing different.

This book is about changing all that. It outlines the many ways you can be different while avoiding the lure of those things that sound different but really aren't.

With this in hand, you should be in a better position to thrive in a very unforgiving and competitive world. It's a book, if you'll pardon the pun, that can make a difference in your business.

JACK TROUT

CONTENTS

CHAPTER 1. The Tyranny of Choice   1

CHAPTER 2. Whatever Happened to the U.S.P.?   11

CHAPTER 3. Reinventing the U.S.P.   19

CHAPTER 4. Quality and Customer Orientation Are
            Rarely Differentiating Ideas   27

CHAPTER 5. Creativity Is Not a Differentiating Idea   37

CHAPTER 6. Price Is Rarely a Differentiating Idea   45

CHAPTER 7. Breadth of Line Is a Difficult Way
            to Differentiate   57

CHAPTER 8. The Steps to Differentiation   65

CHAPTER 9. Differentiation Takes Place in the Mind   73

CHAPTER 10. Being First Is a Differentiating Idea   83

CHAPTER 11. Attribute Ownership Is a Way
            to Differentiate   95

CHAPTER 12. Leadership Is a Way to Differentiate   107

CHAPTER 13. Heritage Is a Differentiating Idea   115

CHAPTER 14. Market Specialty Is a Differentiating Idea   127

CHAPTER 15. Preference Is a Differentiating Idea   135

CHAPTER 16. How a Product Is Made Can Be
             a Differentiating Idea   145

CHAPTER 17. Being the Latest Can Be a
             Differentiating Idea   155

CHAPTER 18. Hotness Is a Way to Differentiate   163

CHAPTER 19. Growth Can Destroy Differentiation   169

CHAPTER 20. Differentiation Often Requires Sacrifice   179

CHAPTER 21. Being Different in Different Places   187

CHAPTER 22. Maintaining Your Difference   195

CHAPTER 23. Who Is in Charge of Differentiation?   205

Notes   213

Index   219

The Tyranny
of Choice

In the beginning, choice was not a problem. When our earliest ancestor wondered "What's for dinner?" the answer wasn't very complicated. It was whatever animal in the neighborhood he could run down, kill, and drag back to the cave.

Today you walk into a cavernous supermarket and gaze out over a sea of different types and cuts of meats that someone else has run down, killed, dressed, and packaged for you.

Your problem is no longer catching it. Your problem is to try to figure out what to buy of the hundreds of different packages staring back at you in the case. Red meat? White meat? The other white meat? Make-believe meat?

But that's only the beginning. Now you have to figure out what part of the animal you want. Loin? Chops? Ribs? Legs? Rump?

And what do you bring home for those family members who don't eat meat?

Fishing for Dinner

Catching a fish for that early ancestor was simply a matter of sharpening a stick and hoping to get lucky.

Today it can mean drifting into a Bass Pro Shop or an L.L. Bean or a Cabela's or an Orvis and being dazzled with a mind-boggling array of rods, reels, lures, clothing, boats, you name it.

At Bass Pro's 300,000-square-foot flagship store in Springfield, Missouri, they will give you a haircut and then make you a fishing lure out of the clippings.

Things have come a long way from that pointed stick.

Going to Dinner

Today many people figure it's better to have someone else figure out what's for dinner. But figuring out where to go is no easy decision in a place like New York City.

That's why, in 1979, Nina and Tim Zagat created the first restaurant survey in New York City to help us answer that difficult question of choice.

Today the pocket-size *Zagat Surveys* have become best-sellers, with 100,000 participants rating and reviewing restaurants in more than forty major U.S. and foreign cities.

An Explosion of Choice

What has changed in business over recent decades is the amazing proliferation of product choices in just about every category. It's been estimated that there are 1 million SKUs (standard stocking units) out there in America. An average supermarket has 40,000 SKUs. Now for the stunner. An average family gets 80 to 85 percent of its needs from 150 SKUs. That means there's a good chance we'll ignore 39,850 items in that store.

Buying a car in the 1950s meant a choice between a model from GM, Ford, Chrysler, or American Motors. Today you have your pick of cars, from GM, Ford, Chrysler, Toyota, Honda, Volkswagen, Fiat, Nissan, Mitsubishi, Renault, Suzuki, Daihatsu, BMW, Mercedes, Hyundai, Daiwa, Mazda, Isuzu, Kia, and Volvo. There were 140 motor vehicle models available in the early 1970s. There are 260 today.

Even in as thin a market as $175,000 Ferrari-type sports cars there is growing competition. You have Lamborghini, a new Bentley sports car, Aston Martin, and a new Mercedes called the Vision SLR.

And the choice of tires for these cars is even worse. It used to be Goodyear, Firestone, General, and Sears. Today you have the likes of Goodyear, Bridgestone, Cordovan, Michelin, Cooper, Dayton, Firestone, Kelly, Dunlop, Sears, Multi-Mile, Pirelli, General, Armstrong, Sentry, Uniroyal, and twenty-two other brands.

The big difference is that what used to be national markets with local companies competing for business has become a global market with everyone competing for everyone's business everywhere.

Choice in Healthcare

Consider something as basic as healthcare. In the old days you had your doctor, your hospital, Blue Cross and perhaps Aetna/US Healthcare, Medicare, or Medicaid. Now you have to deal with new names like MedPartners, Cigna, Prucare, Columbia, Kaiser, Wellpoint, Quorum, Oxford, Americare, Multiplan, and concepts like Health Maintenance Organizations (HMO), Peer Review Organizations (PRO), Physician Hospital Organizations (PHO), and Preferred Provider Organizations (PPO).

It's gotten so confusing that magazines like *U.S. News & World Report* have taken to rating hospitals and HMOs so as to make our choice easier.

In New York City, a book titled *How to Find the Best Doctors* fills 1,300 pages with the results of surveys sent to 28,000 doctors, nurses, and hospital administrators.

California is even getting into a healthcare public "report card" arena. It started with several physician groups and health plans publishing "report cards" evaluating the performance of network providers. Then the 2.1-million-member PacifiCare of California published its new "Quality Index" report on its Web site, rating more than 100 physician-based organizations according to clinical outcome measures, as well as member satisfaction, administrative data, and professional/organizational data.

It's gotten so confusing that people aren't worrying about getting sick. They worry more about where you go to get better.

Choice Is Spreading

What we just described is what has happened to the U.S. market, which, of the world's markets, has by far the most choice (because our citizens have the most money and the most marketing people trying to get it from them).

Consider an emerging nation like China. After decades of buying generic food products manufactured by state-owned enterprises, China's consumers now can choose from a growing array of domestic and foreign brand-name products each time they go shopping. According to a recent survey, a national market for brand-name food products has already begun to emerge. Already China has 135 "national" food brands from which to pick. They've got a long way to go but they are on their way to some serious tyranny.

Some markets are far from emerging. Countries like Liberia, Somalia, North Korea, and Tanzania are so poor and chaotic that choice is but a gleam in people's eyes.

The Law of Division

What drives choice is the law of division, which was published in *The Twenty-two Immutable Laws of Marketing.*

Like an amoeba dividing in a petri dish, the marketing arena can be viewed as an ever-expanding sea of categories.

A category starts off as a single entity. Computers, for example. But over time, the category breaks up into other segments. Mainframes, minicomputers, workstations, personal computers, laptops, notebooks, pen computers.

Like the computer, the automobile started off as a single category. Three brands (Chevrolet, Ford, and Plymouth) dominated the market. Then the category divided. Today we have luxury cars, moderately priced cars, and inexpensive cars. Full-size, intermediate, and compacts. Sports cars, four-wheel-drive vehicles, RVs, minivans, and suburbans, which are station wagons on steroids.

In the television industry, ABC, CBS, and NBC once accounted for 90 percent of the viewing audience. Now we have network, independent, cable, satellite, and public television. Today a wired household has over 150 channels from which to choose. And they are threatening us with "streaming video" that promises to make the cable industry's dream of a 500-channel universe look pathetically unambitious. With all that, if you flip through the channels and try to find something to watch, by the time you find it the show will be over.

"Division" is a process that is unstoppable. If you have any doubts, consider the table on the explosion of choice.[1]

The Explosion of Choice

Item	Early 1970s	Late 1990s
Vehicle models	140	260
KFC menu items	7	14
Vehicle styles	654	1,212
Frito-Lay chip varieties	10	78
SUV styles	8	38
Breakfast cereals	160	340
PC models	0	400
Pop-Tarts	3	29
Software titles	0	250,000
Soft drink brands	20	87
Web sites	0	4,757,894
Bottled water brands	16	50
Movie releases	267	458
Milk types	4	19
Airports	11,261	18,202
Colgate toothpastes	2	17
Magazine titles	339	790
Mouthwashes	15	66
New book titles	40,530	77,446
Dental flosses	12	64
Community colleges	886	1,742
Prescription drugs	6,131	7,563
Amusement parks	362	1,174
OTC pain relievers	17	141
TV screen sizes	5	15
Levi's jean styles	41	70
Houston TV channels	5	185
Running shoe styles	5	285
Radio stations	7,038	12,458
Women's hosiery styles	5	90
McDonald's items	13	43
Contact lens types	1	36

The "Choice Industry"

All this has led to an entire industry dedicated to helping people with their choices. We've already talked about Zagat's restaurant guides and healthcare report cards.

Everywhere you turn, someone is offering advice on things like which of the 8,000 mutual funds to buy. Or how to find the right dentist in St. Louis. Or the right M.B.A. program from among hundreds of business schools. (Will that help me get a Wall Street job?)

The Internet is fast filling up with dot coms that can help you find and select anything you can imagine, all promised at rock-bottom prices.

Magazines like *Consumer Reports* and *Consumers Digest* deal with the onslaught of products and choices by rotating the categories on which they report. The only problem is that they go into so much detail that you're more confused than when you started.

Consumer psychologists say this sea of choices is driving us bonkers. Consider what Carol Moog, Ph.D., has to say on the subject: "Too many choices, all of which can be fulfilled instantly, indulged immediately, keeps children—and adults—infantile. From a marketing perspective, people stop caring, get as fat and fatigued as foie gras geese, and lose their decision-making capabilities. They withdraw and protect against the overstimulation; they get 'bored.'"[2]

Choice Can Be Cruel

The dictionary defines *tyranny* as absolute power that often is harsh or cruel.

So it is with choice. With the enormous competition, markets today are driven by choice. The customer has so many good alternatives that you pay dearly for your mistakes. Your competitors get your business and you don't get it back very easily. Companies that don't understand this will not survive. (Now that's cruel.)

Just look at some of the names on the headstones in the brand graveyard: American Motors, Burger Chef, Carte Blanche, Eastern Airlines, Gainesburgers, Gimbel's, Hathaway shirts, Horn & Hardart, Mr. Salty pretzels, Philco, Trump Shuttle, VisiCalc, Woolworth's.

And this is only a short list of names that are no longer with us.

You Have to Be Careful

If you ignore your uniqueness and try to be everything for everybody, you quickly undermine what makes you different. Consider Chevrolet. Once the dominant good-value family car, Chevrolet tried to add "expensive," "sporty," "small," and "truck" to their identity. Their "differentness" melted away as did their business. The brand is now behind Honda, Ford, and Toyota (Honda, 735,633 cars; Toyota, 679,626 cars; Ford, 591,010 cars; Chevrolet, 479,802 cars; total sales in 1998).

If you ignore changes in the market, your difference can become less important. Consider DEC (Digital Equipment Corporation). Once America's premier minicomputer manufacturer, they ignored changing technology that was making desktop computing the driving force in the office. Their "differentness" became less important. DEC is now deceased, having been absorbed by Compaq, one of the biggies in desktop computing.

If you stay in the shadow of your larger competitors and never establish your differentness, you will always be weak. Consider Westinghouse. They never emerged from the shadow of General Electric. Today Westinghouse is no longer with us. Or consider Goodrich. Over the years, Goodrich could reinvent the wheel and Goodyear would get all the credit. Because of the name confusion with their larger competitor, it was all but impossible to separate themselves in the minds of their prospects. Today Goodrich is on life-support systems.

It's an unforgiving world out there.

And It Will Only Get Worse

Don't bet that all this will calm down. We feel that it will get worse for the simple reason that choice appears to beget more choice.

In a book entitled *Faster*, author James Glieck outlines what can only be called a bewildering future which he describes as, "The acceleration of just about everything." Consider the following scenario that he describes:

> This proliferation of choice represents yet another positive feedback loop—a whole menagerie of such loops. The more information glut bears down on you, the more Internet "portals" and search engines and infobots arise to help by pouring information your way. The more telephone lines you have, the more you need. The more patents, the more patent lawyers and patent search services. The more cookbooks you buy or browse, the more you feel the need to serve your guests something new; the more cookbooks you need. The complications beget choice; the choices inspire technology; the technologies create complication. Without the distribution and manufacturing efficiencies of the modern age, without toll-free numbers and express delivery and bar codes and scanners and, above all, computers, the choices would not be multiplying like this.

Ladies and gentlemen, we haven't seen anything yet.

Whatever Happened
to the U.S.P.?

In 1960, an advertising agency chairman named Rosser Reeves was known as the high priest of hard sell. He wrote a very popular book titled *Reality in Advertising*. His book was translated into twenty-eight languages and was widely used as a college textbook. In many ways it was the beginning of modern-day marketing.

In his book he introduced and defined a concept called the unique selling proposition, or U.S.P. for short.

The Definition

To Rosser, U.S.P. was a precise term so he gave it a three-part definition:

1. Each advertisement must make a proposition to the consumer. Not just words, not just product puffery, not just show-window

advertising. Each advertisement must say to each reader: "Buy this product, and you will get this specific benefit."

2. The proposition must be one that the competition either cannot, or does not, offer. It must be unique—either a uniqueness of the brand or a claim not otherwise made in that particular field of advertising.

3. The proposition must be so strong that it can move the mass millions (i.e., to pull over new customers to your product).[1]

He went on to say that most advertising in that day was "the tired art of puffery." There was no real message. Copywriters who did not understand reality wrote these advertisements.

Well, you might think that this was an argument of the past and that Mr. Reeves's ideas have long been accepted by today's advertising practitioner.

Wrong.

The Argument Still Rages

What's stunning is that the argument still rages on Madison Avenue. A front-page article in *Advertising Age* that was published thirty-seven years after Mr. Reeves's book proclaimed:

"Poets vs. killers": Perpetual ad debate—stress art or stick to hard sell?—is reaching fever pitch with fortunes hanging in the balance.[2]

This article, that went on for pages, laid out the battle of the creatives that see their work as artful and emotional and the marketers who want advertising that is factual and rational.

One group wants to bond with the customer. The other group wants to sell the customer.

It's time we stopped arguing and faced not reality in advertising but reality in the marketplace.

Where's Rosser Now That We Need Him?

When Mr. Reeves was talking about being different, the world was an easy place. Global competition didn't exist. In fact, by today's standards, real competition barely existed.

The concept of being unique or different is far more important in the year 2000 than it was in 1960.

While "to sell or not to sell" arguments have been raging, the New World Order has suddenly arrived. Today many companies have bigger sales than many countries have gross national products. The top 500 global companies now represent 70 percent of the world's trade.

Mergers and acquisitions are everywhere as the rich get richer and bigger. Not only is there more competition, there is tougher and smarter competition.

What this new competition is often able to exploit is the fact that buying behavior isn't just about people and income, it's also about how dissatisfied consumers are with present alternatives.

Step 1 in Building Brands

There are books and books on branding but very few books talk much about differentiation. And if it does get mentioned, rarely do authors go much beyond talking about the fact that branding is important to do.

Consider Young & Rubicam, a very large and talented global advertising agency that has developed a system they call "brand science." They say that "differentiation is first." It defines a brand and distinguishes it from all others. It is how brands are born and how they die as differentiation declines. (We do believe they've got it.)

But rather than really get into the subject, they quickly segue to things like relevance, esteem, knowledge, and brand power grids.

Well, good readers, we plan on going further. If differentiation is about the life and death of a brand, we feel it's worth your while to explore this subject in depth. (Good old Rosser would have wanted it that way.)

The Importance of Being Different

Choosing among multiple options is always based on differences, implicit or explicit. Psychologists point out that vividly differentiated differences that are anchored to a product can enhance memory because they can be appreciated intellectually. In other words, if you're advertising a product, you ought to give the consumer a reason to choose that product. If you can entertain at the same time, that's great.

Unfortunately, the fact is that many advertising people don't appreciate the need to offer the prospect a unique selling proposition.

Most of these people feel that selling isn't cool and that people only respond to companies that don't try to sell them. Besides, many will argue, there often isn't enough "difference" to talk about in the products. What they ignore is the fact that, whether or not people like to be sold, in a sea of choice a prospect still has the problem of figuring out what to buy or not to buy. In other words, alternatives are but the raw material of decision making. And decisions must be made.

How People Figure Things Out

Psychologists think a lot about how people solve problems. They've come up with four functions that come into play: intuition, thinking, feeling, and sensing. People tend to lead their decision-making process with one of these functions. Let's look at these functions from a selling point of view.

Differentiating with "Intuitives"

People who use intuition concentrate on the possibilities. They avoid the details and tend to look at the big picture.

This type of person would be very susceptible to a differentiating strategy based on your product being the next generation in its category. When the makers of Advil positioned their new ibuprofen as "advanced medicine for pain," they were differentiating themselves perfectly for the big-picture crowd.

Intuitives are very interested in the possibility of what's coming next. This is why selling to intuitives is often a very effective way to present a new type of product.

Differentiating with "Thinkers"

Thinkers are analytical, precise, and logical. They process a lot of information, often ignoring the emotional or feeling aspects of a situation. While they may appear to be ruthless or uncaring, that isn't really accurate. They are just thinking (Henry Kissinger types).

These people are susceptible to a logical argument of facts about a product. BMW's differentiating strategy of "the ultimate driving machine" probably works very well with this crowd, especially when they present facts like ergonomic design, maneuverability, non-overweight engine, and lots of expert reviews on how BMWs drive.

Differentiating with "Feelers"

Feelers are interested in the feelings of others. They dislike intellectual analysis and follow their own likes and dislikes. They enjoy working with people and are capable of great loyalty.

This type of person is ideal for third-party endorsements from experts who look and sound real. The Miracle-Gro campaign that differentiates itself as the choice of experts is perfect for feelers. Nice people surrounded by beautiful flowers and talking about the wonders of Miracle-Gro is a perfect strategy.

Differentiating with "Sensors"

Sensors see things as they are and have great respect for facts. They have an enormous capacity for detail and seldom make errors. They are good at putting things in context.

Hertz's differentiating strategy of leadership (there's Hertz and not exactly) is a great program for the sensors, who instinctively know that Hertz is indeed number one. (Twenty-five years of telling us they are number one doesn't hurt.) To them it's just common sense that Hertz is the best.

What should be noted is that people often are a mixture of these functions. "Intuitives" and "feelers" both tend to dislike too much detail. "Thinkers" and "sensors" work with more information. But they all are trying to make a decision on what to buy, one way or another.

You Can Differentiate Anything

Theodore Levitt, the Harvard marketing guru, wrote a book titled *The Marketing Imagination.* He was definitely on Rosser Reeves's side when he stated in chapter 4 of his book that you can differentiate anything.

His point is that products must be augmented by offering customers more than they think they need or have come to expect. This could be with additional services or support. General Electric does this by advising customers on the nuances of doing business around the globe. GE also added service capability so its customers didn't have to keep service people on staff.

Otis Elevator uses remote diagnostics as a way to differentiate itself. In high-traffic office buildings, where servicing elevators is a major inconvenience to occupants and visitors alike, Otis uses its remote diagnostics capabilities to predict possible service interruptions. It sends employees to carry out preventive maintenance in the evening, when traffic is light.

Oral-B created a powerful source of differentiation with a toothbrush that tells customers when they need a new one (a patented blue dye in the center bristles).

Differentiating Commodities

Even the world of meats and produce has found ways to differentiate itself and thus create that unique selling proposition. Their successful strategies can be summed up in five ways:

1. *Identify.* Ordinary bananas became better bananas by adding a small Chiquita label to the fruit. Dole did the same for pineapple with the Dole label, as did the lettuce people by putting each head into a clear Foxy lettuce package. Of course, you then have to communicate why people should look for these labels.

2. *Personify.* The Green Giant character became the difference in a family of vegetables in many forms. Frank Perdue became the tough man behind the tender chicken.

3. *Create a new generic.* The cantaloupe people wanted to differentiate a special, big cantaloupe. But rather than call them just plain "big," they introduced a new category called Crenshaw melons. Tyson wanted to sell miniature chickens, which doesn't sound very appetizing. So they introduced Cornish game hens.

4. *Change the name.* Sometimes your original name doesn't sound like it would be something you would want to put in your mouth. Like a Chinese gooseberry. By changing it to kiwifruit, the world suddenly had a new favorite fruit it wanted to put in its mouth.

5. *Reposition the category.* Pork was just pig for many years. All that did was conjure up mental pictures of little animals wallowing in the mud. Then they jumped on the chicken bandwagon and became "the other white meat." A very good move when red meat became a perceptual problem.

Where there's a will, there's a way to differentiate.

Reinventing the U.S.P.

osser Reeves had the will to differentiate.

But forty years ago, the way to differentiate was usually based on a tangible difference between products. Usually it included a benefit that could be dramatized by a comparison with competitors.

"It cleans your breath while it cleans your teeth," said Colgate dental cream. (Years later, Crest added decay-fighting ingredients to toothpaste and preempted that U.S.P.)

"Stops BO," proclaimed Lifebuoy soap in the 1950s. Actually, all soaps stop body odor, but Lifebuoy got there first and grabbed that claim. (More on this point later.)

"Our bottles are washed with live steam" was a point of differentiation from legendary copywriter Claude Hopkins, who had toured his client's brewery. (Once again, every brewery was doing the same thing. But he was the first to claim the high ground of hygiene.)

Simple science was on the side of many companies in those days. Anacin, for instance, could tout its unique "combination of ingredients" as superior to plain aspirin or aspirin with buffers. Physicians could explain that the combination of Anacin's particular ingredients had different effects on the human body than aspirin alone.

What Happened?

Today it's a lot tougher to hang onto a U.S.P. or a product difference or benefit. As a result, most marketers have drifted toward other concepts.

Partly, that's because of the torrent of new products. They cloud the mind with conflicting claims and teeny points of difference. ("Now! Tartar control with the great taste of fresh mint gel.")

Partly, it's because the number one competitive response is usually me-tooism. Competing products are becoming more and more alike. Technology enables competitors to tear apart, reverse engineer, and knock off product features even before you have the chance to establish your uniqueness.

Partly, it's because of speed. Think of a company like Intel, which increases data storage and performance each year at astounding rates. Think of the diaper business, where new products race to market in as little as six months. Most companies don't have time to rest on their laurels.

When you survive by reinventing yourself every other day, it's tough to differentiate on a product difference alone.

Is It Really "New?"

In 1987, there were 14,254 new products introduced in the United States, according to the reporting firm of Market Intelligence Service Ltd.

By 1998, the number had grown to 25,181.

To put that number in context, it means sixty-nine new products surfaced every day of the year. Or that every city, town, village, and hamlet in America could host its very own new product. ("Welcome to Buford City, home of Buttermilk shampoo.")

But in new products, quantity doesn't mean quality. The overwhelming majority of this deluge of lotions and potions and widgets aren't breakthroughs of any kind. They're just bells, whistles, and tweaks.

Michael Lasky has watched the new product scene for twenty-one years. He's a patent lawyer with Merchant & Gould in Minneapolis. "Most new products are minutiae," he says. "They are not true inventions, which is what a patent really is. They are just insignificant, trivial advances. And that makes it much easier for a competitor to come out with their own 'flavor beads' or 'triple edge' or whatever."[1]

So much for your special product feature.

Is It Really Protected?

Patent protection can be quite strong, assuming you have the breadth and scope of a breakthrough invention. (Even some surgical operations have been patented.) Or you can surround yourself with enough new gizmos to keep competitors at bay.

Consider the $4 billion diaper wars, where as many as 1,000 patents (and about as many lawyers) guard everything from the Velcro fastener tabs to the amount of elastic around the legs. Believe it or not, the diaper biz is one of the most heavily patented in the annals of the Patent and Trademark Office.

The two big rivals in diaper land, Procter & Gamble and Kimberly-Clark, even agreed to stop suing each other and cross-license a variety of disputed patents. Together, they already control three-quarters of the diaper market. Now they can clobber their much smaller competitors with royalty payments for special "cuffs" that stop those annoying diaper leaks.

So, Bunkie, do you feel lucky today? Are you ready to barge into the battle for baby's bottom with your new product? If so, then get ready for one ugly rash when the big boys unload their patents and lawyers on you.

But here's a pleasant surprise. This sort of predatory patenting and gonzo lawyering is the exception, not the rule.

"Throughout the consumer-product business," observes *The Wall Street Journal*, "manufacturers of lower-priced house brands routinely skate close to the edges of a patent as they attempt to copy new ideas without stealing them outright."[2] These are the knock-offs, look-alikes, and taste-alikes.

One British marketing professor puts it this way: "The last few demanding years have drilled into us all the vital need to innovate to gain a competitive edge. But when we really do steal a lead, we find the advantage is only temporary. Why? Because our competitors have been working to the same pressures, usually with similar resources."[3]

How do they do it? Powerful new computer technologies let them dismantle your new idea, millimeter by millimeter, and then replicate it.

Analyzing Them to Death

Sometimes the mania to analyze and tear apart the competition can literally tear them apart. The unique point of difference, if there ever was one, never has a chance.

Robert McMath is a former Colgate-Palmolive executive, now a consultant. He likes to tell the story of what happened when a shampoo called Wash & Comb hit test markets. It promised to eliminate tangles. Competitors were extremely interested. Then McMath swung into action.

"My consulting firm alone purchased 3,000 bottles in the Atlanta market," he says. "As a result, Wash & Comb looked like a sure winner. But real people weren't buying it. Other marketers were. It bombed when it rolled out nationally."[4]

The same thing happened when Hunt-Wesson, which owns popcorn prince Orville Redenbacher, went out to "study" a new brand called Cracker Jack Extra Fresh popping corn. First, they cleaned out the store shelves. Then they went directly to the Grand Union warehouse to purchase by the case, again and again. (An executive at the supermarket commented that they were just about the only people buying the product.)

It's no surprise that Cracker Jack Extra Fresh flopped when it went national. Hunt-Wesson stopped buying it.

It's Not Impossible

We didn't say product differentiation was an impossible way to differentiate. We just said it was difficult.

Every few years, Gillette reinvents shaving. They did it with two-bladed razors (Trac II), adjustable two-bladed razors (Atra), shock-absorbent razors (Sensor), and now with three-bladed razors (Mach 3).

On the surface, the Mach 3 is just a new product.

Underneath, though, is the excruciating hard work and passion of a company that regularly obsoletes its most recent best-seller.

The Mach 3 required an investment of $750 million before a single new blade was sold. A thicket of thirty-five patents surrounds the product, including "progressively aligned" blades, comfort edges for less "drag," and an advanced "forward pivot" action. (Sounds more like a Ferrari than a curved stick to scrape off whiskers.)

The result of all this invention and effort? A market share in wet shaving that borders on antitrust. Now that's differentiation.

Improve, Upgrade, and Reinvent

Same company, same technique, different product.

Oral-B toothbrushes hadn't introduced a new toothbrush in the twenty-seven years before Gillette acquired it.

Gillette put a team of 150 people into researching manual plaque removal. The result was a stream of new products including a floss made with a proprietary fiber, and its top-of-the-line Advantage toothbrush.

If you're thinking of the product feature route to differentiate, you would be wise to study the Gillette model. Improve, upgrade, and reinvent.

In other words, go big, or don't bother going at all.

What often happens is that companies take their eye off their difference. Volvo has pioneered the concept of safe cars as their product difference. They've introduced a number of safety ideas such as modular construction, side-door air bags, and running lights. But in recent years, they were late with the safety of front-wheel drive and four-wheel drive.

Now, while the Japanese are beginning to talk about new electronic safety devices, Volvo is into sporty convertibles and coupes that don't look safe. They are taking their eye off what has made them different.

Hot Chicken and Cool Music

Spicy chicken is a hot new product. Popeyes Chicken serves up Cajun-style fried chicken that is zesty, to say the least. "We're out to save America from bland chicken," say their TV commercials.

Popeyes' $12 million ad budget is puny compared to its giant competitor, the Colonel.

But its product feature is a red-hot point of difference—enough to drive them past Church's Chicken and Chick-Fil-A into the second sales slot in chicken restaurants behind KFC.

The Bose Wave radio is another big idea. "It seems small," says the advertising, "until you turn it on."

It's a radio unlike any other. Smaller than a breadbox, it produces rich, room-filling sound. How? The sound travels through a patented seven-foot acoustic waveguide speaker, folded inside the device. This nifty product brought Bose, already regarded as one of the most respected names in the sound business, a Best of What's New award from *Popular Science*.

Sales are brisk, even at $349 a pop. Last time we checked the Bose Web site, the order form advised, "Due to overwhelming demand, please allow 4 to 6 weeks for delivery."

Beyond Product and Benefit

Will competitors get their arms around spicy chicken and cool sounds? Most likely, if you accept the conclusion of three British professors. Writing in *The Journal of Advertising Research*, they argue:

> Me-tooism remains the dominant force in competition. Being competitive means cashing in on one's competitors' successes. Such imitation is not just restricted to minor product developments (baking soda in toothpaste or guaranteed-money-back long-term investments), but applies even more to the major product characteristics (all mainstream cars have to be speedy, safe, fairly economical, etc.).[5]

As you can see, inventing and then hanging on to a truly different product is hard work. But it can be done.

Ted Levitt's Warning

Returning to one of the fathers of marketing, Harvard's Ted Levitt had some very strong things to say on this subject in his 1991 book titled *Thinking About Management*:

> Differentiation is one of the most important strategic and tactical activities in which companies must constantly engage. It is not discretionary. And everything can be differentiated, even so-called "commodities" such as cement, copper, wheat, money, air cargo, marine insurance.
>   There is no such thing as a commodity, only people who act and think like commodities. Everything can be differentiated, as just observed, and usually is. Think only of soap, beer, investment banking,

credit cards, steel warehousing, temporary help services, education. There is no reason for any company to get stuck in the commodity trap, forever confined to competing totally on price alone. Historically, companies that have taken and stayed resolutely on the commodity path, even when they have driven their costs deeply down, have become extinct.

In the chapters ahead, we'll explore a dozen ways to do it, and we'll broaden the field to consider services as well as products.

But first, a few yellow caution flags.

There are some ideas that look appealing, but will rarely differentiate you.

Quality and Customer Orientation Are Rarely Differentiating Ideas

If you live or work in New Jersey, you have your choice of hundreds of banks. Megabanks such as Chase, midsize players such as Commerce, community banks such as Columbia Savings. How do consumers choose a place to plunk down their assets?

Into this fray, and onto the radio, comes the voice of Bob Cox, president of $20 billion Summit Bank. Here is his pitch:

> We're always looking for better ways to serve you.
> No customer is too small to listen to.
> No employee is too big to listen.
> We're reaching higher.

Sorry, Bob, but these ideas are no salvation in a hypercompetitive world. Your competitors have read the same books and taken the same courses.

For the customers of the Summit Banks of the world, reasonable quality and service are an expectation, not a tiebreaker.

In other words, quality is a given these days, not a difference. Knowing and loving your customer is a given, not a difference.

The War on Quality

Yes, the 1990s witnessed a war on quality. Business leaders demanded tools and technique to measure it. An army of gurus and academics marched forth with books and endless diatribes on how to define, predict, and ensure this elusive creature called quality.

On they came, a numbing maze of acronyms and buzzwords: the Seven Old Tools, the Seven New Tools, TQM, SPC, QFD, CQL, and just about any other combination of three letters you could string together.

In 1993 alone, there were 422 books in print with "Quality" in their title. Today, there are half as many. (We must have won the war.)

Survey after survey today acknowledges that consumers see quality improvements all around them. Cars that are better made. Small appliances that last longer. Computers with instruction manuals in simple English.

The editorial director at polling firm Roper Starch Worldwide explains it this way: "All brands have to work harder to get ahead today. They keep upping the ante to meet consumers' needs. The consumer is still king. And it doesn't look like the equation is going to change anytime soon. Consumers have not slacked off in their demands as the economy has improved. If anything, they've grown more demanding."[1]

Who Wins with Quality?

Who among us doesn't appreciate a better-made product, or a zero-defects guarantee?

But does quality pay? Ah, the jury is still out on that one.

A Gallup survey done for the American Society for Quality Control found that only 28 percent of executives interviewed say they achieved significant results from their quality initiatives. ("Significant" is defined as increasing profitability or market share.)

A similar study done by the British Department of Trade and Industry revealed that in 86 percent of the firms examined, the design and implementation of advanced manufacturing systems failed to realize any improvements in quality, flexibility, or due-date performance. Even worse, 43 percent of these companies did not improve their overall competitive position.

But just try lowering your quality and competing in today's world. Good luck. The customer's expectation isn't going away, no matter how much it costs you to keep pace.

The War for Customer Satisfaction

If quality were a war, then the assault on the customer would be Armageddon.

A landmark study published in *Harvard Business Review* argued that companies could improve profits by at least 25 percent just by reducing customer defections by 5 percent. Whoa, Nellie. You could hear the alarm bells going off in boardrooms across the land.

Seminars, books, and counselors told us 1,001 ways to dazzle, love, partner with, and just plain hang on to that person called a customer.

We were told the customer is a collaborator. The customer is the CEO. The customer is king. The customer is a butterfly. (Don't even ask.)

Customer feedback meant every complaint was a gift. Better after-marketing would keep a customer for life. Learn how to manage in total customer time.

It was enough to drive you into the not-for-profit world.

As the century rolled over, *Marketing Management* concluded, "Practically every company today is geared up to satisfy its customers. 'We do whatever it takes' is the everyday refrain."[2]

These are the exceptions, of course. Like the nation's airlines, flying as high as the stock market with record numbers of passengers in 1999. It's not boom times for their passengers, however. Complaints are mounting over overbooking, scant leg room, mishandled baggage, incomplete or misleading information about delayed flights, and frustration with frequent flier miles that are easy to accumulate but next to impossible to use.

Love Those Miles

In 1983, American Airlines introduced its AAdvantage program. Back then, the airline actually believed mileage rewards would:

1. Encourage brand loyalty.
2. Bring in the competition's customers who wanted better deals.
3. Differentiate American from United and everyone else.

AAdvantage now boasts 29 million members worldwide, including half a million in Brazil alone. What management did not anticipate was the stampede by competitors to respond in kind, and the virtual impossibility of stopping such a program once under way.

Today everybody gives away miles. Let's say you fly a lot around the Hawaiian Islands. Your miles will get you an Aloha Pass on

Aloha Airlines. Flying to Bangkok on business? Thai Airways has its Royal Orchid program.

Wait a minute. Airlines are supposed to sell tickets, not give them away. Frequent flier programs, supposedly a customer service bonanza, have had the unwanted effects of:

- Reducing demand for some paid tickets.
- Limiting available seats for popular vacation spots like Hawaii.
- Irritating good customers who can't cash in their miles.

Here is the reluctant conclusion of Leonard Berry, professor of marketing and director of retailing studies at Texas A&M University: "What they have not done is differentiate the sponsoring airlines for the frequent travelers to the degree that justifies the costs and drawbacks. The frequent traveler concept, essentially pricing benefits for better customers, is simply too easily imitated."[3]

The Rising Tide

A more savvy and more demanding consumer raises the level for every marketer.

Now the local bagel shop has a frequent nosher program. (Half a dozen sesame bagels? Here, let me punch your card.)

An obscure CD ordered from an obscure Internet address comes with a money-back guarantee. (And they honor it.)

A California HMO publishes a report card that rates hundreds of physician groups according to their clinical outcomes and patient satisfaction. (Those in the top 10 percent are starred as "best practices.")

Is this a great time to be a consumer, or what?

Just ask a major bank in Seattle, which found its retail customers had become much less tolerant of delays in answering complaints or resolving disputes. Some in-depth interviews revealed the reason: Nordstrom. The hometown department store chain, with its famously obsessive level of customer service, had changed the mindset of bank customers as well. Imagine you're the bank. What do you tell your customers? "Oh, that's how Nordstrom does it. Remember, we're just a bank."

If the customer already expects more, then knock-your-socks-off service doesn't get you into the end-zone. It just keeps you in the game.

And by the way, all your competitors are trying to make love to your customers, too.

The Myth

Even scoring high on the vaunted Malcolm Baldrige National Quality Award criteria, or actually winning a Baldrige award, is itself no guarantee of success. Baldrige award winners have seen their stock prices fluctuate, experienced product development delays, and lost money on new ventures.

The great myth of marketing in the 1990s was that "serving the customer" was the name of the game.

Many marketing people live in a dream world. They believe in the fantasy of the virgin market. This is the belief that marketing is a two-player game involving just the company and the customer. In this fantasy, a company develops a product or service designed to appeal to customer needs, and then uses marketing to harvest the crop.

But there are no virgin markets. The reality of marketing is that a market consists of consumers strongly or weakly held by a range of competitors. A marketing campaign, therefore, consists of holding on to your customers while at the same time attempting to take customers away from your competitors.

That's what differentiation can do. It's not just about knowing your customer. It's about your customer knowing about you.

Satisfaction versus Commitment

One other point: Customer satisfaction is not the same as customer commitment.

Research from Quality Institute International Inc. shows that:

- More than 40 percent of customers who claimed to be satisfied switched suppliers without looking back. (So many choices, so little time.)
- Eighty-nine percent of people who owned cars from a certain manufacturer said they were very satisfied, and 67 percent said they intended to purchase another car from that manufacturer.
- But fewer than 20 percent actually did so.

All those lovable customers you've been busy courting? They can and will double-cross you.

Consider what's happening to Nordstrom, the king of service. In an April 19, 1999, *Business Week* article, the headline reads "Great Service Wasn't Enough." The article talked about Nordstrom's weak sales growth, disappointing profits, and volatile stock performance. It blamed overexpansion.

But William E. Nordstrom put it this way: "We have not been able to keep up with the changing needs of the customers."

Bill, you've been double-crossed.

Michael Porter Gets "On Board"

He may be the most famous Harvard Business School professor of all time, and he's had lots to say over the years about differentiation.

In his latest collection of essays, titled *On Competition*, Michael Porter finally puts quality and customer passion in their place. He does it by drawing a line between operational effectiveness and strategic positioning.

Operational effectiveness means simply performing better the same activities your competitors perform. This can be a source of short-run competitive advantage, but in the long run it's nowhere near sufficient.

As companies race to benchmark each other, Porter observes, companies become more alike.

Instead, he says, companies need to position themselves differently from their competition. That means finding a point of differentiation unique (and meaningful) in their industry.

"Operational effectiveness means you're running the same race faster," Porter says. "But strategy is choosing to run a different race because it's the one you've set yourself up to win."[4]

Professor Porter has seen the light.

But It Can Happen

At the beginning of this chapter, we said that quality and customer orientation are rarely a way to differentiate yourself.

Midwest Express Airlines is such a "rarely."

They are a very successful regional airline that has truly made service and customer orientation their differentiator.

They have free coffee and newspapers at the gates. Steak and shrimp dinners. Chocolate chip cookies. Friendly flight attendants. No jammed seating. And best of all, it's all for basic coach fare. Now for the trick: They focus on filling their seats with corporate commuters instead of bargain-hunting, book-in-advance leisure travelers.

How Come It Works?

Desperate for profits, the major airlines now worry about service for only the dozen or so people in first class. The industry has jammed its planes, moving as many passengers as possible through often-inconvenient hubs.

And despite all this, raised its basic fares sharply.

All this has infuriated the basic business traveler, who suddenly has fallen in love with Midwest Express and their direct flights.

So the moral about service as a differentiator: You can indeed use this as a strategy. But only if your competition is stupid enough to let you.

Creativity Is Not a Differentiating Idea

In his book *Reality in Advertising*, Rosser Reeves railed against what he saw as puffery and ineffectual advertising. Concepts like "rich with true caramel flavors," "the best taste ever," and "It's incredibly smooth" incurred his verbal wrath.

While not up to his standards of selling, at least they were an attempt to sell. One wonders how he would have reacted to today's advertising that doesn't even make the attempt. Consider these concepts plucked from a few magazines: "Start something." "Welcome aboard. Really." "Changing the world with great care." "People drive us." "Expanding possibilities."

The Creativity Trap

Puffery has been replaced with vagueness. A large amount of today's advertising has gotten so creative or entertaining that it's sometimes hard to tell what companies are even advertising.

Consider this full-page advertisement from J.P. Morgan, a leading global financial adviser, underwriter, and lender.

The advertisement has no headline, just a human face staring out and a block of copy that reads: "I have never settled for better when best was within reach. I have zero interest in okay. I have never mistaken listening for understanding. I have frustrated cynics. I have been difficult when necessary. I have been easy when faced with perfection. I have lit fires. I work for J.P. Morgan."

What Makes J.P. Morgan Different?

This is a nice set of thoughts and a nice piece of prose. But what in the world is J.P. Morgan trying to sell the readers of *Fortune* magazine? That they are a company that publishes insightful messages from employees? That their people try harder? Beats us. Besides, we're not giving our money to some unknown employee, we're giving it to a large, successful organization.

What makes J.P. Morgan different is anything but vague. It's their 150-year-old heritage of serving the world's most prominent corporations, governments, and wealthy families. J.P. Morgan helped structure and finance General Electric and AT&T in their infancy. It loaned money to the French and the British during two world wars. It propped up Mexico with $2.6 billion in bonds and the Russian Federation with the same amount.

What they should be running is a program that presents their unique capabilities in the context of their long heritage: "Generating wealth for 150 years." (Starting with old J.P. Morgan himself.)

And what prospective client doesn't want some wealth generated?

An Industry Debate

This vagueness has gotten so bad that *Advertising Age* reported the fact that some company CEOs are receiving letters from stockholders about shareholder equity being wasted by "commercials that appeared utterly removed from the real world task of attempting to convince a viewer to buy the product."[1]

Rance Crain, the editor in chief of *Advertising Age*, has been on a crusade against vague, ineffectual advertising that is being run under the guise of being creative. His point, and it's a good one, is that poor work costs advertising the CEO support that it needs.

It used to be that a CEO would wonder which half of his advertising budget was being wasted. Now he is beginning to wonder if it's the whole budget.

It's no wonder that a survey commissioned by the American Advertising Federation showed lukewarm support for advertising as a tool to help companies grow.

When executives were asked whether they were satisfied with their companies' advertising efforts, just 6.8 percent replied they were very satisfied.

The "Creativity" Defense

What's driving the advertising industry toward a cliff is the belief of many that advertising is losing its effectiveness in an age of over-communication and cynicism.

These advocates of artful, poetic advertising point to a time in the '60s when advertising underwent a big change. It was a time when the element of "likeability" became important. Before that, you told somebody that this thing would cure a headache and this thing would go fast or get good mileage. It was about logic and selling. Their view is that if it sells too hard, the message not only won't be liked, it will be ignored.

That's why they strive to run advertising that's emotional or provocative or funny or cool—advertising that forms a "bond" with the consumer.

Shelly Lazarus, the chairwoman of the American Association of Advertising Agencies, addressed her associates at their eighty-first annual meeting in 1999. She urged her members to celebrate the unconventional and the unexpected—the better to meet competition from the likes of management consultants who are threatening to usurp the traditional role agencies play in marketing communications.

"My management consultant friends sometimes seem almost offended by the irrational and illogical," Lazarus said. "Have you noticed that?"

By contrast, she asserted, "we thrive on that," because "consumers are often irrational and illogical," influenced by "intangible emotional values that often transcend logic."[2]

The Ghost of Bill Bernbach

If you challenge this thinking, many will evoke the ghost of Bill Bernbach, a very famous ad man who started the likeable advertising revolution in the '60s.

They point to his work as being the beginning of the creative revolution. Unfortunately, as with most revolutions, it went very wrong as the years rolled on.

Bill Bernbach and Rosser Reeves weren't really very far apart in their efforts. It's just that their style was different. Bernbach took powerful selling ideas and simply presented them in everyday language that didn't take the product too seriously. He simply introduced more reality into advertising.

Creative Differentiation

If you look at Bill Bernbach's work today, you'll find that it was brilliant strategy, simply expressed and very logical.

"Think small" for Volkswagen was a wonderful way to differentiate the Beetle from the large, heavily chromed patrol boats that Detroit was offering the public.

"Because we're only number two in rent-a-cars, we try harder" for Avis was an honest way to differentiate itself from Hertz and the other rent-a-cars all trying to put you in the driver's seat.

"You don't have to be Jewish to enjoy Levy's Jewish rye bread" was a straightforward way to reposition this rye bread as a great bread for everyone. (Its Jewishness made it different. He had to make this difference more attractive to those who weren't Jewish.)

Yes, this is an age where advertising is not as effective as it once was. Yes, this is an age where there are too many products chasing the same consumers. But if Bernbach were still plying his trade, he would be writing advertising that is warm, human, and above all, right-on strategy.

The Ghost of Mean Joe Greene

The one idea that you hear a great deal about today is using emotion to be different. Program after program has emotional scenes of people kissing people or people kissing babies or people being people. The product plays a minor role in these tableaux of life.

If you question that approach, many will point to the very famous Coca-Cola commercial that featured the Pittsburgh Steelers lineman Mean Joe Greene and a little seven-year-old who shared a Coke with him after the game. It was a heart-tugging commercial that was loved by all. Unfortunately, while it made great viewing, it didn't sell any Coca-Cola. (At the time, Pepsi's differentiating idea as the "choice of the new generation" was in high gear.)

But that's a detail which was quickly passed over by the emotion lovers in the business. So let's address this issue, but on a scientific basis (not on an emotional basis).

Emotion and Choice

To get to the bottom of this argument, we went to the world of psychology to determine how emotion and reason figure in our ability to make choices.

There's a great deal of complex and heavy material on the subject of why, of all creatures on earth, humans are the most emotional.

Richard and Bernice Lazarus, two professors of psychology at the University of California, caught our eye. In a book titled *Passion and Reason* (Oxford University Press, 1994), they explode many myths about emotions. One is that emotions are irrational and do not depend on thinking and reasoning. Their point: Emotion and intelligence go hand in hand. (So much for Shelly Lazarus.)

Another important point they make is that emotions always depend substantially on reason. Their point: Emotion depends on an appraisal of personal meaning. Without meaning, without appraisal, there is no emotion.

This means that if an advertisement presents emotion and leaves out a reason to buy, all that emotion is a waste of money. There will be no appraisal. (So much for Mean Joe Greene.)

Another psychologist, Dr. Carol Moog, put it very well: "Strictly emotional behavior, broadly speaking, occurs in very young children or severely cognitively impaired adults. Realistically assessed, rationally considered attributes, to a greater or lesser degree, contributes to all choices, and to all points of differentiation, regardless of the emotional pull, loyalty, or arousal properties of products."[3]

In other words, you have to give a person a reason to buy your product.

We rest our case.

Sergio Gets Religion

Sergio Zyman is the former marketing guru of Coca-Cola who is now a consultant to companies in search of a strategy. And he suddenly sounds amazingly like us. He says company marketing should be more concerned about selling the product than jingles or signing up celebrities.

For those of you who are not familiar with his track record, he was involved with New Coke, or what we call the Edsel from Atlanta.

He was around when Coke's ultimate differentiating idea, "the real thing," was abandoned for a number of meaningless slogans.

He was on the scene when Coke went off to Hollywood to get some advertising that was the ultimate in creative nonselling unless you consider polar bears drinking Coke a differentiating idea. (The cola that polar bears prefer.)

He says that "advertising is supposed to communicate the benefits and differences of a brand." (Attaboy, Sergio.) And that marketing "is a discipline, a science that positions your product in relative terms to your competition." (Absolutely.)

Then he has the chutzpah to say that agencies "peddle the thought that advertising is an art, when it's not."[4] (How come you bought a lot of that "art" for Coke?)

Well, we're happy to see that Sergio has had a late-life conversion. It's too bad Sergio's realization didn't come sooner, as it would have saved Coke a bundle of money on those bad decisions in his earlier life.

Information, Not Ads

While Sergio now gets it, many advertising people fail to understand that their job is to present important information about a product and why a person should buy it. And that information shouldn't look too much like an ad.

Minds are limited as to how much information they will take in and store (more in Chapter 9).

One way of overcoming the mind's natural stinginess when it comes to accepting new information is to work hard at presenting your message as important news.

Too many advertisements try to entertain or be clever. In so doing they often overlook the news factor in their story.

The Starch research people can demonstrate that headlines that contain news score better in readership than those that don't. Unfortunately, most creative people see this kind of thinking as old news.

If people think you've got an important message to convey, generally they'll open their eyes or ears long enough to absorb what you've got to say.

In the coming chapters, we'll outline many different ways you can differentiate a product or company. In each case, the method presented represents important news about a product. Whether it's an attribute, leadership, heritage, preference, or any other tried-and-true approach, they all represent important information that should be helpful in dealing with that problem of choice.

The trick is not to bury that information in what some call "creativity."

CHAPTER 6

Price Is Rarely a Differentiating Idea

Price is often the enemy of differentiation.

By definition, being different should be worth something. It's the reason that supports the case for paying a little more—or at least the same—for a product or service.

But when price becomes the focus of a message or a company's marketing activities, you are beginning to undermine your chances to be perceived as being unique. What you're doing is making price the main consideration for picking you over your competition. That's not a healthy way to go.

Few companies find happiness with this approach for the simple reason that every one of your competitors has access to a pencil. And with it, they can mark down their prices any time they want. And there goes your advantage.

As Michael Porter says, cutting prices is usually insanity if the competition can go as low as you can.

The Case of Cheaper Carrots

To support Porter's premise, we point you to a start-up company that came up with a unique packaging system for baby carrots. It was one that produced a decided price advantage over the two big suppliers already in the business.

To get on the supermarket shelves, they entered the market not with better carrots but with a better price. Instantly the two big suppliers matched the upstart's price. This only forced the new company to go lower, which once again was matched by the established brands.

When a board member asked the management of this start-up to predict what would happen, the management predicted that the two big companies would not continue to reduce their prices because it was "irrational." They were losing money because of their older packaging technology.

The board member called us about this prediction. We advised that it was perfectly rational. Why would the two companies that dominated the market make it easy for a new company with a manufacturing price advantage to get into the market? They were quite happy with things the way they were.

At the next board meeting, the start-up company management was encouraged to sell their new manufacturing system to one of the established brands. Which they did for a nice profit.

Everyone was happy and another low-price strategy bit the dust.

Building a Price Advantage

We did not say that a price strategy as a differentiator was impossible, only difficult.

Southwest Airlines has used low price to differentiate itself. But it has done so by, in CEO Herb Kelleher's words, "being different."

By using one kind of airplane they saved on training and maintenance costs. By offering no advanced seats they avoided expensive reservation systems. By offering no food they eliminated expense and time. By avoiding expensive hub airports and using less expensive smaller airports they avoided high gate charges.

By being different, Southwest has been able to construct a system with the lowest cost per air mile than any other airline. Unfortunately, this did turn them into a bit of a cattle car. But to offset this they work very hard at making the trip more fun. (The attendants do stand-up comedy.)

They have differentiated themselves as the low-fare airline. And they have become big enough that they can't be forced out of a market by a bigger airline lowering their prices. Many airlines have tried to imitate Southwest, and most have failed.

The Wal-Mart Success

One could say that "everyday low prices" has worked for Wal-Mart in the mass-merchandising business. As with Southwest Airlines, they have been able to make low price a meaningful differentiating idea. But consider how they got there.

First, they began their efforts in America's C&D counties (the ones with smaller populations) where their competition was the small mom-and-pop general merchandise stores. That was like the German war machine running through the Balkans. Very little resistance.

Then they began to build their technology base along with their new store openings. As their volumes grew they added "supplier muscle" to their weapons. While the going has been tougher in areas where Kmart, Target, and Costco also reside, they now indeed have that structural cost advantage to support their claim.

Dell's Approach

Dell Computer has certainly used price as a weapon to carve out a sizeable piece of the computer business. With over $18 billion in sales, it has challenged Compaq for leadership in PC sales.

Its unique approach was to avoid retailers and go direct to users with a lower price proposition. They attacked IBM and Compaq with comparative ads featuring side-by-side photos of computers. Copy under a Dell PC: "The lap of luxury" with a $3,899 price tag on the screen. Under a Compaq model: "The lap of lunacy" with a $7,699 price.

Compaq sued but wouldn't give up its expensive distribution system. The result was more and more market share headed toward Dell.

Ironically, while price was the initial weapon, Dell's business has changed greatly. It is far less reliant on product-and-price ads. Today much of Dell's business comes from relationships with large corporate customers who place orders through dedicated Dell reps and through customized Web commerce sites that Dell offers corporate buyers.

Charles Schwab's Approach

So it is with Charles Schwab, the company that was the first discount broker. It was their price approach that broke the hammerlock that the big full-service brokers had on the market. But this only gave way to an army of other discount brokers, who were more recently followed by an army of yet cheaper brokers on the Internet.

Like Dell, Charles Schwab has moved to the high ground with more and more service. While they still are about discounts, if you look at their advertising, Charles Schwab looks more and more like Merrill Lynch than Merrill Lynch, the behemoth of costly full-service, looks like Merrill Lynch.

The moral of both Dell and Charles Schwab is that you can start with price but without a structural advantage you can't finish with price. You've got to move up the food chain.

Getting Around Price

Market leaders will always be attacked on price. It appears to be almost a law of nature. So what do you do? Do you have to match all their moves that are made against you?

Well, there are some tried-and-true methods of getting around a price attack:

1. Do something special. The leader can go to its biggest customers and offer something special. Nike went to Foot Locker with Tuned Air, a $130 running shoe that they make exclusively for the big shoe retailer. So far so good. Foot Locker has ordered more than a million pairs and expects to sell $200 million worth. That's comparable to what it did with the best-selling Air Jordans.

2. Cause some confusion. In some industries, pricing can be quite complicated. Such is the case with telephone rates. Some years ago, MCI launched their Friends & Families discount program. The deal was discounts on those calls you made to your friends and families as well as to those that were made to you. All you had to do was sign up with the names and phone numbers of those on your list. AT&T ignored this for a while, but MCI's market share started to climb. Eventually, AT&T came down off their mountain and introduced "MCI math." This aggressive advertising program challenged those MCI rates as not being very much when you got past the small print. (Their 20 percent discount shrunk to about 6 percent, which worked out to pennies on a phone call.) As the arguments raged, all that really happened was that the market became confused about what was a real discount and what wasn't. Other discounts from Sprint and a new breed of telephone discounters only added to the confusion. MCI's market share progress was halted. Who wins when the market is confused? You guessed it: the leader. People just figured, "Why bother? Let's stay with AT&T."

3. Shift the argument. Another good strategy in a pricing battle is to introduce the concept of total cost as opposed to initial cost. In some categories, the costs you incur after you buy a product can be substantial. If your product performs better after the purchase, you might be able to build a cost-for-cost ownership versus cost-of-purchase argument. A variation on this is the concept of longevity. An expensive product, such as a Mercedes, can have a high price but it will last far longer than your average car. That's a nice rationale to get customers over what could be a bad case of

sticker shock. A similar strategy can be used to sell expensive beds such as Duxiana, which go for $3,000 or more. The concept: You spend a lot more time in your bed than in your expensive car. In fact, you spend about 40 percent of your life in bed. So why scrimp?

Some Words about Promotions

Finally, do price promotions do much for a brand? Some extensive international work has shown that sales generally go back to where they were once a short-term price promotion is over. The promotion lasts while it lasts. This has long been suspected but only recently systematically tested. The hope has often lingered with management that there might be a positive aftereffect, at least in their case.

It is now known that this is not so, and why: A promotion is taken up virtually only by the brand's long-term or "loyal" customers. The evidence shows that people seldom buy a strange brand just because its price is cut. They simply avoid paying more than they have to when one of their customary and familiar brands is temporarily on sale.

This is why there are no aftereffects on sales: A promoted brand does not hang on to any new customers who might have first bought it during the sales blip, because there were virtually no such "new customers" to speak of. What is more, a typical short-term promotion reaches only a few of the brand's existing customers, say 10 or 20 percent. Yet promotions are very costly, and additionally they have costly side effects on production and distribution logistics.

No Long-Term Effects

Promotions do not seem to leave memory traces. ("What brand had 20 cents off six or so months ago?") Consumers seem to accept that prices are sometimes cut (even for a BMW, say, or air miles for first class).

Large-scale promotions now occur even though management has traditionally sought to stop its salespeople from cutting the price. ("The only way I could nail the sale, sir.") Marketing management itself now cuts the price, and even seems proud of it. Nonetheless, price promotions must generally be run at a loss, otherwise there would be even more of them. And the bigger the promotional blip, the bigger the loss. So why is so much spent on price promotions? Senior management would like to cut its promotional budget but does not usually know how to. The exception was the unknown CEO who said, "All you need is guts."

The Attractions of Promotions

Without a doubt, there are some things that a short-term price promotion can accomplish. Here's the most popular list of reasons we have heard:

- Shift stock (by "giving the product away").
- Help catch up on a missed sales target (at a cost).
- Postpone losing shelf space (until the next threat).
- Buy extra shelf space (for a time).
- Satisfy the trade (for a time).
- Help keep up with the competition. ("They did it last week.")
- Have something to do (instead of going to see the agency).

David Ogilvy on Price

David Ogilvy, a legend alongside the likes of Rosser Reeves and Bill Bernbach, has some strong words to say about deals and price. They are certainly worth repeating:

> Any damn fool can put on a deal, but it takes genius, faith and perseverance to create a brand.

The financial rewards do not always come in next quarter's earnings per share, but come they do. When Philip Morris bought General Foods for five billion dollars, they were buying brands.

There used to be a prosperous brand of coffee called Chase & Sanborn. Then they started dealing. They became addicted to price-offs. Where is Chase & Sanborn today? Dead as a doornail.

The manufacturers who dedicate their advertising to building a favorable image, the most sharply defined personality for their brand, are the ones who will get the largest share of market at the highest profit.

The time has come to sound an alarm! To warn what is going to happen to brands if so much is spent on deals that there is no money left to advertise them.

Deals don't build the kind of indestructible image which is the only thing that can make your brand part of the fabric of American life.[1]

As you can see, David Ogilvy also believed in being different.

A Low Price in Siberia

It might shock you, but Coke and Pepsi are getting hammered by a local soft drink company called Crazy Cola in Krasnoyarsk, Russia. AC Nielsen Russia has them at a 48 percent share of cola sales volume.

The reason is price. At a local grocery, a 2-liter bottle of Coke or Pepsi costs the equivalent of 77 U.S. cents; a 1.5-liter bottle of Crazy Cola is 39 cents. The premium price is beyond the reach of most consumers.

With these problems, Coke is expected to operate in Russia at about 50 percent of capacity in 1999. Pepsi took a $218 million charge to restructure its Russian business.

The question is: Can the Russian cola hang in there when times get better? As *The Wall Street Journal* reported, Coke and Pepsi can only hope that Victoria Pimenova, a twenty-five-year-old graduate student here, is a representative consumer. Pimenova keeps her eye on the Western brands and hopes one day to be able to afford them again. "Crazy Cola is fun, and it's our local product," she says. "But it's a drink for people who don't have money. Coke and Pepsi taste better."[2]

The Travails of Sports Retailing

Among the full-line retailers in this $46 billion industry, the four biggest publicly held companies are losing money. Jumbo Sports (once known as Sports and Recreation) is on its way to dying. Just for Feet of Birmingham, Alabama is closing a large chunk of its 236 stores and reorganizing under Chapter 11 bankruptcy.

Sports Authority, by far the biggest, has seen its stock swoon and is struggling to turn itself around.

The problem, in a nutshell, is that if you live by price, you can die by price—especially in an industry that is overpopulated by sports retailers both on-line and of the bricks and mortar variety.

None of these establishments is differentiated nor do they have unique merchandise to sell. That leaves them with just "price" as their strategy. This isn't much of a weapon when you have to take on the likes of Wal-Mart and Kmart which now account for 35 percent of all sporting goods sales.

Unfortunately, a lot of these folks won't stay in the game for very long.

The Ultimate Price: Free

What is truly amazing today is the rush of Internet firms that, in an effort to boost traffic, have adopted no-charge policies. There are free e-greetings or e-faxes, a dozen companies offering free e-mail, five offer free computers, others offer free software. They figure they'll eventually make money by running ads for paying customers. Hopefully, something will turn up.

It's becoming a fact of Internet life. "Time and again, do-it-for-free companies are coming in and spoiling an industry for everyone else," says venture capitalist David Cowan in a recent *Wall Street Journal* article. "And if you don't give it away, some other start-up will."[3]

Can any of these for-free companies ever make money on advertising or purchases online? That question is still very much up in the air. But one thing is perfectly clear. As long as venture capitalists and the stock market keep shoveling money at Internet businesses, entrepreneurs are going to try ever more daredevil approaches to build a business.

Good luck.

Differentiating with High Price

We're far more impressed with companies that use a high price to help differentiate themselves.

Joy perfume announces that it's the "costliest perfume in the world." There are two important principles at work here:

1. *High-quality products should be more expensive.* People expect to pay more for a better product, but the quality should be visible in some way. A jar of Orville Redenbacher gourmet popping corn looks a lot more impressive than a less expensive can of Jolly Time. It also promises the benefit of popping almost all of the kernels.

    If I'm paying more for a NorthFace outdoor jacket, it's helpful if I have that GoreTex label hanging on it that says "guaranteed to keep you dry." My Rolex should look sturdy and substantial. But, to be honest, a lot of watches at a fraction of the Rolex price look sturdy and substantial. This raises the next point.

2. *High-priced products should offer prestige.* If I've spent $5000 for a Rolex, I want my friends and neighbors to know I'm wearing a Rolex. It's how they know I'm successful. So it is

with expensive cars. While they will never admit it, the reason people spend $50,000 for a car is to impress their friends
and neighbors.

Therein lies the reason why the Cadillac Allante was
a $50,000 bomb. Would my neighbors be impressed with a
"Cadillac"? Where's the prestige? How will my neighbors
know I spent $50,000 for an automobile?

What does a high price say about the product? It says the product
is worth a lot. In essence, the high price becomes an inherent benefit of the product itself. (This is one of the powerful motivating
factors in the success of many high-end flanking moves—Mercedes-
Benz automobiles, Absolut vodka, Grey Poupon mustard, to name
three examples.)

CHAPTER

7

Breadth of Line Is a Difficult Way to Differentiate

As we discussed in the opening chapter, people are overwhelmed by choice. This results in the fact that the average person has trouble making choices about buying decisions.

But for some businesses, the big selection does work as a differentiator. Charles Lazarus, founder of Toys "R" Us, says, "When parents have no clear idea of what to buy, they go to the store with the biggest selection."

Category Killers

"Biggest selection" has become the big mantra in retailing. But this has become a moving target. Superstores, or "category killers," as they are lovingly referred to, have become kings of the hill in the industry. These superstores have become successful by using an everything-under-one-roof approach and deep discounts to cater to different niches. Toys "R" Us led the superstore wave that is now populated by the likes of Home Depot, Lechters, Staples, Auto Zone, PetSmart, and their superstore competitors.

But now we find that the superstores are under attack by very specialized full-line stores. These stores carve out narrow, profitable segments of the superstores' businesses. Noodle Kidoodle is an example that caters to the upscale educational toy market.

Enter the Discounters

As with price, the problem of using "breadth of line" as a differentiator is that there is no way to keep your competitors from using the same strategy.

The discounters are using their size and buying power to increase their emphasis on some product categories. Wal-Mart, for example, has opened up large toy sections in its stores.

Here are a few examples of just how ugly it has gotten in the land of retail:

- *Baby Superstore* came up with a winning idea: Sell everything for babies under one roof. Now Toys "R" Us has created the knock-off Babies "R" Us, and discounters like Target are wading in, all of which puts pressure on Baby Superstores' earnings.

- *CompUSA* cut into the sales of the computing departments of small electronics and office supply stores. Now electronics superstores, office supply superstores, mail-order houses, and other computer superstores are selling computers, and the price competition has made margins razor thin.

- *Sports Authority* put many regional sports stores out of business. But now the Kmart unit is finding more growth difficult in this mature market segment, where many competitors are trying to emulate its formula.

- *Party City* made the party sections of local stores seem anachronistic. But just as it went public, copycats appeared. Now discount stores like Wal-Mart are offering party supplies for less, and other superstores like Garden Ridge, a home decorator, have opened giant party sections in their stores.

How Big Is Too Big?

Ironically, the breadth-of-line concept that made many of these stores different is now turning into a nightmare.

First there's the problem of managing the endless selection of SKUs crammed into these giant boxes called stores. Watch some poor salesperson at Home Depot trying to find the right item in cartons that are 25 feet overhead. It's something to behold. The computer might say it's there, but finding it is another matter.

Then there is the issue of alienating core consumer groups. While the die-hard bargain hunter may relish the allure of discovery amid a maze of aisles, less driven shoppers often find the same format frustrating or intimidating.

Growing legions of time-short Americans have opted for pricier quick-hit trips to convenience stores and strip malls. This is especially true for single shoppers who don't want to waste precious after-work time or weekend hours in a store.

Older consumers are often turned off by the prospect of parking on the fringes of a huge parking lot and then having to lug bulky packages back to the car.

Younger parents with cranky kids in tow don't have the time to figure out a bewildering store layout.

Becoming More Shopper Friendly

The behemoth category killers are now wrestling with the problems of being too big. Some are reducing SKUs and making their interiors more approachable with better lighting, wider aisles, and lower shelves.

Others are into trying to create a festive shopping experience by adding entertainment, fast food, interactive displays, anything to entice people to hang around for a while and, hopefully, to buy a little more.

While variety is the spice of life, too much spice will lead to heartburn.

Home Depot Junior

One of the most interesting efforts to attract those customers who are intimidated by "too big" is Home Depot's scaled-down test stores called Villager's Hardware.

Modeled after the small hardware store and other home improvement chains, this store aims to attract customers who aren't willing to brave the cavernous Home Depot stores for modest fix-it jobs.

Yet at 40,000 square feet (about one-third the size of a Home Depot), the Villager's Hardware might still be a little too big for a zip-in and zip-out affair.

But it sure is an interesting experiment that could hammer another nail in the coffin of the limited-line, independent hardware stores.

Breadth of Line on the Web

If you think retail stores have taken choice too far, the Internet has quickly become an infinite supply of goods and services. It's "choice" not to a new level but to a new realm.

eToys, Inc., for example, has added children's books to the toys and other kids' products it carries. This means that eToys now offers more than 100,000 different products. (How's that for a full line of kids' products?)

Of course the move into books puts them in competition with Amazon and other online booksellers. Which of course is tit for tat, as Amazon has also launched into toys, electronics, CDs, and whatever else they can sell.

In the Web game, it appears that you can quickly find yourself surrounded with online competitors saying to themselves, "We can sell that." And the next day, they do.

Cybersqueeze

Since every online player can quickly amass a breadth of line, this is no longer a point of differentiation.

So where do they head next? You guessed it: price. And as you learned in Chapter 6, this is not an easy way to differentiate yourself. Especially in a medium where your customers can compare price with but a few keystrokes on their computer. (There's no having to go back into your car to drive to another store.)

The bottom line is grim. Even the biggest players such as Amazon are yet to make a profit. It's becoming, as *The Wall Street Journal* announced, "A site-eat-site world."

A Digital Gold Rush?

All this reminds us of the gold rush days in California: everyone rushing off to get rich in the Internet mountains.

But there just might be an important lesson in the history of this event. The people who made the real money in the gold rush were those who sold the maps, the tools, and the clothing. (It's where Levi's started.)

Most of the folks who rushed off to get rich never did. And what's worse, a fair percentage didn't make it back alive.

Our guess is that the equipment manufacturers as well as the legion of consultants designing the Web sites and fancy interfaces will make most of the gold.

What's Really Needed

As the Web becomes an infinite supply of goods and services, what people will really need is guidance on what and where to buy. Sort of a Zagat's for everything, which would be a site consisting entirely of consumer opinions and reviews of anything you can buy.

But then there's the question of how this site could make money and how it would be organized. Restaurants are one thing but wading into the Internet is another. All that information would be tough to swallow.

An Important Lesson

What the retail and Web world demonstrates is the fact that all differentiators are not created equal.

Breadth of line is nowhere near as strong a differentiator as things such as leadership or preference or product difference. The reason is that it can be easily copied by a competitor. This leaves you with very little maneuvering room other than price.

This is why, when working with clients, we often try to use this concept as a stepping-stone to a differentiator with more longevity. Such was the case of a retailer in New England.

From "Full Line" to "Preference"

One retailer that has been successful in using breadth of line as a differentiator is a large furniture store in Rhode Island called Alperts Furniture Showplace. But they used it as a stepping-stone to building a unique selling proposition around preference, which is a better differentiator (see Chapter 15).

First, they built a very large store that was able to accommodate a very large selection of furniture. This enabled them to sell more furniture out of one location than any other store. This set up the following case for shopping at Alperts. The copy is straight out of a radio commercial.

> Getting a good value is one thing. But getting good value on a lot of good things is what makes a store truly successful. And that's what Alperts is all about. People come for a good deal, but what really surprises them is the amazing selection of furniture of all kinds under one roof.
>
> As a result, we sell more fine furniture in one store than our competition sells in all their stores combined. The way we figure it, if you don't find what you're looking for, we haven't done our job.
>
> That's why Alperts has become Rhode Island's favorite furniture store.

As Hershel Alpert would probably say, "Upon this breadth of line, I built my preference story." And it's a wonderful story that saw his business increase dramatically. Alperts is indeed Rhode Island's favorite place to buy furniture.

CHAPTER

8

The Steps to Differentiation

This chapter explains, for the first time, a process we've developed over our thirty years in the differentiating business. It's not about being creative or cute or imaginative. It's all about logic, which is a science that deals with the rules and tests of sound thinking.

The Power of Logic

A trip to a dictionary will define a *logical* argument as one that is cogent, compelling, convincing, valid, clear. It shows skill in thinking or reasoning.

Now doesn't that sound like an argument you would like to have to support what you're trying to sell? You'd better believe it.

And yet, how many logical arguments do you come across in the marketing world? Very few.

That lack of logic is at the heart of most programs that fail. On the other side of the coin, if you can see the logic in the argument, chances are you've got a winner.

If Avis is only number two in rent-a-cars, then it figures that they have to try harder. It's not creative, it's logical.

If IBM's size covers all aspects of computing, then it's logical that they can integrate all the pieces better than any other manufacturer. Integrated computing is what makes them different.

Creativity versus Logic

Since logic is a science, it's logical that constructing a unique selling proposition should be a science, not an art. And yet the creative faction fights this idea tooth and nail. They hate the thought of being locked into a process that limits their creative musing.

But what's worse is to see a company go through the strategy process and come up with a straightforward logical argument for their brand, then turn it over to the creative folks and watch the argument disappear in a cloud of singing and dancing.

Once, while working with a bank on their strategy, we discovered that they were the leader in Small Business Administration loans in their trading area. Most of those loans, it turned out, were going to recent immigrants starting businesses in America. People pursuing the American dream of success.

The recommended strategy was logical and direct. What made this bank different was that it was "the home of the American dream."

Everyone liked the idea, and it was handed over to an agency for implementation. When we saw it again it had become "We bank on your dreams."

So much for logic and a differentiating idea.

To avoid this, you have to make sure that everyone follows a simple, four-step process.

Step 1: Make Sense in the Context

Arguments are never made in a vacuum. There are always surrounding competitors trying to make arguments of their own. Your message has to make sense in the context of the category. It has to start with what the marketplace has heard and registered from your competition.

What you really want to get is a quick snapshot of the perceptions that exist in the mind, not deep thoughts.

What you're after are the perceptual strengths and weaknesses of you and your competitors as they exist in the minds of the target group of customers.

Our favorite mode of research is to line up the basic attributes that surround a category and then ask people to score them on a rating scale of 1 to 10. This is done on a competitor-by-competitor basis. The objective is to see who owns what idea or concept in a category. That's the context for your argument.

The context also includes what's happening in the market. Is the timing for your idea right?

Nordstrom's differentiating idea of "better service" played perfectly into the context of a department store world that was reducing its people and service as a way to cut costs.

Lotus launched the first successful network on "groupware software" called Notes just as corporate America was networking its PCs.

It's like riding a wave. If you're too early or late you'll go nowhere. Catch it just right and you'll get a long and profitable ride for your difference.

Step 2: Find the Differentiating Idea

To be different is to be not the same. To be unique is to be one of its kind.

So you're looking for something that separates you from your competitors. The secret to this is understanding that your differentness does not have to be product related.

Consider a horse. Yes, horses are quickly differentiated by their type. There are racehorses, jumpers, ranch horses, wild horses, and on and on. But, in racehorses you can differentiate them by breeding, by performance, by stable, by trainer, and on and on.

Consider a college. America has too many colleges and universities: 3,600 more than anywhere else in the world. They are similar in many ways, especially in their willingness to take government aid for grants and student loans.

Hillsdale College, 90 miles west of Detroit, has come up with a unique selling proposition to its conservative constituency by declining all of Uncle Sam's dollars, even for federally backed loans. (Very few of its competitors can do this.)

Hillsdale's pitch: "We're free from government influence." They reinforce this concept by positioning the college as a mecca for conservative thought.

As one fund-raiser commented, "This is a product we can sell." And they have the numbers to prove it.

There are many ways to set your company or product apart. The coming chapters cover this in far more detail. Let's just say the trick is to find that difference and then use it to set up a benefit for your customer.

Step 3: Have the Credentials

To build a logical argument for your difference, you must have the credentials to support your differentiating idea, to make it real and believable. Earlier we mentioned IBM. Their size was the key credential in setting up "integrated computing."

If you have a product difference, then you should be able to demonstrate that difference. The demonstration, in turn, becomes your credentials. If you have a leak-proof valve, then you should be able to have a direct comparison with valves that can leak.

Claims of difference without proof are really just claims. For example, a "wide-track" Pontiac must be wider than other cars. British Air as the "world's favorite airline" should fly more people than any other airline. Coca-Cola as the "real thing" has to have invented colas. When it's "Hertz and not exactly" there should be some unique services that the others don't offer.

You can't differentiate with smoke and mirrors. Consumers are skeptical. They're thinking, "Oh yeah, Mr. Advertiser? Prove it!" You must be able to support your argument.

It's not exactly like being in a court of law. (Although you might have to prove every claim if you get challenged by the FTC or the TV networks.)

It's more like being in the court of public opinion.

Step 4: Communicate Your Difference

Just as you can't keep your light under a basket, you can't keep your difference under wraps.

If you build a differentiated product, the world will not automatically beat a path to your door. Better products don't win. Better perceptions tend to be the winners. Truth will not out unless it has some help along the way.

Every aspect of your communications should reflect your difference. Your advertising. Your brochures. Your Web site. Your sales presentations.

We have a client in the fast-food world who sends Christmas cards to his franchisees. The CEO called with the complaint that his card didn't have his differentiating idea in it. We suggested that it was Christmas and maybe he could skip it. He retorted, "No. I want it in the card." Needless to say, his difference went out along with his Christmas greetings.

The bottom line: You can't overcommunicate your difference.

A real differentiating idea is also a real motivational tool. When Avis said, "We're only number two. We try harder," their people took it to heart. They were proud to be underdogs.

When we did the "fast moving bank" for United Jersey Banks some years ago, their employees caught the spirit. They wanted to be faster than their big-city rivals (whom we called Lethargic

National Bank). They wanted to be faster in approving loans and resolving complaints. They saw the value in being more responsive to their customers.

There's a lot of hogwash in corporate America about employee motivation. Brought to you by the "peak performance" crowd, along with their expensive pep rallies.

The folks who report to you don't need mystical answers on "How do I unlock my true potential?" The question they need answered is, "What makes this company different?"

That answer gives them something to latch on to and run with.

Real motivation starts with the weapon of a differentiating idea. Then you can challenge your troops to bring it to life (and make it flourish) in sales, product development, engineering, wherever they work.

Some Words about Resources

Having a good differentiating idea is not enough. You have to have the resources to build a communications program that proclaims your difference to the marketplace.

Even the best idea in the world won't go very far without the money to get it off the ground. Inventors, entrepreneurs, and assorted idea generators seem to think that all their good ideas need is professional marketing help.

Nothing could be further from the truth. Marketing is a game fought in the mind of the prospect. You need money to get into a mind. And you need money to stay in the mind once you get there.

You'll get further with a mediocre idea and a million dollars than with a great idea alone.

Advertising Is Expensive

Some entrepreneurs see advertising as the solution to the problem of getting into prospects' minds. Advertising isn't cheap. It cost

$9,000 a minute to fight World War II. It cost $22,000 a minute to fight the Vietnam War. A one-minute commercial on the NFL Super Bowl will cost you almost $2 million.

Steve Jobs and Steve Wozniak had a great idea. But it was Mike Markkula's $91,000 that put Apple Computer on the map. (For his money, Markkula got one-third of Apple. He should have held out for half.)

Ideas without money are worthless. Well . . . not quite. But you have to use your idea to find the money, not the marketing help. The marketing can come later.

Some entrepreneurs see publicity as a cheap way of getting into prospects' minds. "Free advertising" is how they see it. Publicity isn't free. Rule of thumb: 5-10-20. A small public relations agency will want $5,000 a month to promote your product; a medium-size agency, $10,000 a month; and a big-time agency, $20,000 a month.

Some entrepreneurs see venture capitalists as the solution to their money problems. But only a tiny percentage succeed in finding the funding they need this way.

Some entrepreneurs see corporate America as ready, willing, and financially able to get their offspring off the ground. Good luck, because you'll need it. Very few outside ideas are ever accepted by large companies. Your only real hope is finding a smaller company and persuading it of the merits of your idea.

Remember, an idea without money is worthless. Be prepared to give away a lot for the funding.

It Helps to Be Rich

In marketing, the rich often get richer because they have the resources to drive their ideas into the mind. Their problem is separating the good ideas from the bad ones, and avoiding spending money on too many products and too many programs.

Competition is fierce. The giant corporations put a lot of money behind their brands. Procter & Gamble and Philip Morris each spend more than $2 billion a year on advertising. General Motors spends $1.5 billion a year.

Unlike a consumer product, a technical or business product has to raise less marketing money because the prospect list is shorter and media is less expensive. But there is still a need for adequate funding for a technical product to pay for brochures, sales presentations, and trade shows as well as advertising.

Iron Computer Melts Down

Consider the sad story of a computer company with a real difference: PCs for harsh environments such as hot restaurant kitchens.

No one was making hard-as-nails computers, so a gentleman named John Opincar borrowed $50,000 from family and friends and founded Iron Computer.

But he overrelied on a risky initial public offering on the Internet. Not much money was forthcoming and he was unable to do any real marketing. Iron Computer went into bankruptcy with a wonderful differentiating idea.

Money makes the marketing world go around. If you want to be successful today, you'll have to find the money you need to spin those marketing wheels.

CHAPTER
9

Differentiation Takes
Place in the Mind

As you saw in the last chapter, the final step in differentiation was about building a program to make people aware of your difference.

Doing this entails "positioning," a subject we've been writing about since 1969. While many in business use this word, many still don't know the definition of positioning: how you differentiate your product in the mind of your prospect.

So, for those of you who have missed our many books, speeches, and articles on the subject, here's a synopsis of how the mind works and what are the key principles of positioning.

If you understand how the mind works, you'll understand positioning. These principles underpin our differentiating advice in future chapters.

Minds Can't Cope

While the mind may still be a mystery, we know one thing about it that is for certain—it's under attack.

Most Western societies have become totally "overcommunicated." The explosion of media forms, and the ensuing increase in the volume of communications, has dramatically affected the way people either take in or ignore the information offered to them.

Overcommunication has changed the whole game of communicating with and influencing people. What was overload in the 1970s turned into megaload by the turn of the century.

Here are some statistics to dramatize the problem:

- More information has been produced in the last 30 years than in the previous 5,000.
- The total of all printed knowledge doubles every four or five years.
- One weekday edition of *The New York Times* contains more information than the average person was likely to come across in a lifetime in seventeenth-century England.
- More than 4,000 books are published around the world every day.
- The average white-collar worker uses 70 kilograms of copy paper a year—twice the amount consumed ten years ago.

Electronic Bombardment

And what about the electronic side of our overcommunicated society?

Every day, the World Wide Web grows by a million electronic pages, according to *Scientific American,* adding to the many hundreds of millions already online.

Everywhere you travel in the world, satellites are beaming endless messages to every corner of the globe. By the time a child in the United Kingdom is eighteen, he or she has been exposed to 140,000

TV commercials. In Sweden, the average consumer receives 3,000 commercial messages a day.

In terms of advertising messages, eleven countries in Europe now broadcast well over 6 million TV commercials a year. In the United States, the electronic side of overcommunication continues its relentless attack. Experts say that the country will be going from 150 channels of television to 500. (By the time you find something to watch, the show will be over.)

And then there are all those computers, and the much hyped information superhighway, which promises to deliver massive amounts of information to your home via fiber-optic cables, or CD-ROMs . . . or whatever.

All this means that your differentiating idea must be as simple and as visible as possible and delivered over and over again on all media. The politicians try to stay "on message." Marketers must stay "on differentiation."

Minds Are Limited

Marketing people, and the minds of the people they are trying to influence, are often in conflict.

Unfortunately, these arguments are being presented to minds that really aren't up to dealing with all that glorious information.

Our perceptions are selective. And our memory is highly selective. We are cursed with the physiological limitation of not being able to process an infinite amount of stimuli. This means that in a crowded category, your difference might not be enough unless it is a dramatic difference.

Seeing is not akin to photographing the world, merely registering an image. Memory is not a tape recorder that stores information when we turn it on.

How much of your message gets through depends to a large part on what you are selling, according to years of data compiled on readership scores by advertising category.

For instance, an advertisement for footwear is going to be twice as interesting as an ad for floor coverings, regardless of the brand names or benefits.

Similarly, an ad for perfume—almost any perfume—is going to have double the average readership of a furniture ad.

There is even a "no-interest" category where people will remember no brand names. It's caskets. The lead brand is Batesville. But after a few paragraphs, you'll have forgotten this.

These interest levels—these biases—are firmly in place before we even pick up a magazine or newspaper. This is why the first and second brands in the market have an enormous mental advantage over the later entrants. They tend to preempt the most important differences.

Minds Hate Confusion

Human beings rely more heavily on learning than any other species that has ever existed.

Learning is the way animals and humans acquire new information. Memory is the way they retain that information over time. Memory is not just your ability to remember a phone number. Rather, it's a dynamic system that's used in every other facet of thought processing. We use memory to see. We use it to understand language. We use it to find our way around.

So, if memory is so important, what's the secret of being remembered?

When asked what single event was most helpful to him in developing the theory of relativity, Albert Einstein is reported to have answered: "Figuring out how to think about the problem."

Half the battle is getting to the essence of the problem. Generally speaking this means having a deep understanding of your competition and their place in the mind of your prospect.

It's not about what you want. It's about what your competition will let you do.

The Power of Simplicity

The basic concept of some products predicts failure. Not because they don't work, but because they don't make sense. Consider Mennen's vitamin E deodorant. That's right, you sprayed a vitamin under your arm. It doesn't make sense unless you want the healthiest, best-fed armpits in the nation. It quickly failed.

Consider the Apple Newton. It was a fax, beeper, calendar keeper, and pen-based computer. Too complex. It's gone and the much simpler Palm Pilot is an enormous success.

The best way to really enter minds that hate complexity and confusion is to oversimplify your message.

Some of the most powerful programs are those that focus on a single word. (Wells Fargo: fast. Volvo: safety. Listerine: germ killing.)

The lesson here is not to try to tell your entire story. Just focus on one powerful differentiating idea and drive it into the mind.

That sudden hunch, that creative leap of the mind that "sees" in a flash how to solve a problem in a simple way, is something quite different from general intelligence.

If there's any trick to finding that simple set of words, it's one of being ruthless about how you edit the story you want to tell.

Anything that others could claim just as well as you can, eliminate. Anything that requires a complex analysis to prove, forget. Anything that doesn't fit with your customers' perceptions, avoid.

Minds Are Insecure

Pure logic is no guarantee of a winning argument. As we discussed in Chapter 5, minds tend to be both emotional and rational. Why do people buy what they buy? Why do people act the way they do in the marketplace?

When you ask people why they make a particular purchase, the responses they give are often not very accurate or useful.

That may mean they really do know, but they are reluctant to tell you the right reason. More often, they really don't know precisely what their own motives are.

For when it comes to recall, minds tend to remember things that no longer exist. That's why recognition of a well-established brand often stays high over a long period, even if advertising support is dropped. It's all about the power of being first (see Chapter 10).

In the mid-1980s, an awareness study was conducted on blenders. Consumers were asked to recall all the brand names they could. General Electric came out number two—even though GE hadn't made a blender for twenty years.

Buying What Others Buy

More often than not, people buy what they think they should have. They're sort of like sheep, following the flock.

Do most people really need a four-wheel-drive vehicle? (No.) If they did, why didn't they become popular years ago? (Not fashionable.)

The main reason for this kind of behavior is insecurity, a subject about which many scientists have written extensively. If you've been around a long time, people trust you more and feel secure in their purchase. This is why heritage is a good differentiator (see Chapter 13).

Minds are insecure for many reasons. One reason is perceived risk in doing something as basic as making a purchase. Behavioral scientists say there are five forms of perceived risk:

1. *Monetary risk.* (There's a chance I could lose money on this.)
2. *Functional risk.* (Maybe it won't work, nor do what it's supposed to do.)
3. *Physical risk.* (It looks a little dangerous. I could get hurt.)
4. *Social risk.* (I wonder what my friends will think if I buy this.)

5. *Psychological risk.* (I might feel guilty or irresponsible if I buy this.)

All this explains why people tend to love underdogs but buy from the perceived leaders. If everyone else is buying it, I should be buying it.

Minds Don't Change

It's futile trying to change minds in the marketplace. For example:

- Xerox lost hundreds of millions of dollars trying to convince the market that Xerox machines that didn't make copies were worth the money. No one would buy their computers. But they still buy their copiers.
- Volkswagen's share price dropped over 60 points when they tried to convince the market the VW wasn't just a small, reliable, economical car like the Beetle. No one bought their big, fast cars. They bring back the Beetle and people flock to buy them.
- Coca-Cola blew both prestige and money in an effort to convince the market they had a better thing than "the real thing." No one bought their New Coke. But their Classic version sells as well as ever.

When the market makes up its mind about a product, there's no changing that mind.

As John Kenneth Galbraith once said, "Faced with the choice between changing one's mind and proving that there is no need to do so, almost everyone gets busy on the proof."

Minds Can Lose Focus

Loss of focus is really all about line extension. And no issue in marketing is so controversial.

Companies look at the brands from an economic point of view. To gain cost efficiencies and trade acceptance, they are quite willing to turn a highly focused brand, and one that stands for a certain type of product or idea, into an unfocused brand that represents two or more types of products or ideas.

Look at the issue of line extension from the point of view of the mind. The more variations you attach to the brand, the more the mind loses focus. Gradually, a well-differentiated brand like Chevrolet comes to mean nothing at all.

Scott, the leading brand of toilet tissue, line extended its name into Scotties, Scottkins, and Scott Towels. Pretty soon writing "Scott" on a shopping lest meant very little and Charmin took over the lead. (More on this in Chapter 19.)

Some Surprising Research

With about 70 percent of new products being launched with existing brand names, you would think these companies would have some supporting data on the pluses of line extension. The opposite is true.

The *Journal of Consumer Marketing* noted a large-scale study of 115 new-product launches across five U.S. and U.K. markets.[1] The study compared the market share gained by products launched under established family or corporate brand names with market share gained by products launched under new brand names.

Share was measured two years after each brand's launch. The brand extension products performed significantly less well than the products launched with new brand names.

The *Harvard Business Review* published a study on line extension.[2] Their observations were that, among other things, line extension weakened a brand's image and disturbed trade relations. (More on why this happens in Chapter 19.)

The Power of the Specialist

When you study the marketing wars, the well-differentiated specialist tends to be the winner (see Chapter 14).

Here are some thoughts on why the specialist brand appears to make an impression on the mind.

First, the specialist can focus on one product, one benefit, and one message. This focus enables the marketer to put a sharp point on the message that quickly drives it into the mind.

Domino's can focus on home delivery. Pizza Hut has to talk about its different pizzas, home delivery, and sit-down service.

Another weapon of the specialist is the ability to be perceived as the expert or the best. If that's all they do, they must do it very well.

Finally, the specialist can become the "generic" for the category. *Xerox* became the generic word for copying. ("Please Xerox that for me.") *Federal Express* became the generic word for overnight delivery. ("I'll FedEx it to you.") Even though the lawyers hate it, making the brand name a generic is the ultimate weapon in the marketing wars. But it's something only a specialist can do. The generalist can't become a generic.

CHAPTER
10

Being First Is a Differentiating Idea

Getting into the mind with a new idea or product or benefit is an enormous advantage. That's because, as we described in the last chapter, minds don't like to change.

Psychologists refer to this as "keeping on keeping on." Many experiments have shown the magnetic attraction of the status quo. Most decision makers display a strong bias toward alternatives that perpetuate the current situation.

The bottom line: People tend to stick with what they've got. If you meet someone a little better than your wife or husband, it's really not worth making the switch, what with attorneys' fees and dividing up the house and kids.

And if you're there first, when your competitor tries to copy you, all they will be doing is reinforcing your idea. It's much easier to get into the mind first than to try to convince someone you have a better product than the one that did get there first.

Firsts That Are Still Firsts

Harvard was the first college in America and it's still perceived as the leader.

Time magazine still is the leader over *Newsweek*. *People* leads *US*. *Playboy* is over *Penthouse*.

Chrysler, which introduced minivans, is still the leader in minivans. Hertz, the original rent-a-car company, is still the leader.

Hewlett-Packard leads in desktop laser printers, Sun in workstations, Xerox in copiers. The list goes on and on.

In the mind, the fact that they pioneered the category or product makes them different from their followers. They get a special status because they were the first to the top of the mountain.

This is why Evian, the French water, is spending $20 million in advertising reminding consumers it is *l'original*.

So It Is in Families

Pioneer products are a lot like firstborn children—assertive, highly motivated, often dominant.

Products that aren't first in their category—like later-born children—tend to identify with the underdog and challenge the established order.

(That's why successful later-entry brands tend to be flankers. They differentiate with an uncontested attribute or idea.)

Firstborns grow up knowing they are "bigger, stronger, and smarter than their younger siblings," says MIT scientist Dr. Frank Sulloway. Firstborns should also be more jealous and status conscious and ready to defend their turf, adds Dr. Sulloway, because they've seen their turf invaded by newcomers.[1]

Sulloway, a science historian, spent two decades sifting through more than 2,000 separate studies of birth order and its effects.

Sulloway makes a compelling case that firstborns—whatever their sex, class, or nationality—identify with authority and therefore live to defend the status quo.

It's the same with firstborn companies and products.

Why Firsts Stay Firsts

People feel that the first one is the original and all others are copycats. Being the original translates into more knowledge and more expertise. This is why Coke's "the real thing" resonated so well. (It's an idea that never should have been dropped.)

Studies show that in most cases being first to the market provides a significant and substantial market share advantage over later entrants. It also forces later entrants to find their own distinctive positioning strategy.

Such was the case with Pepsi-Cola's "the choice of the new generation." If Coke was the original, it obviously was for older folks. Pepsi added a little extra sugar and went for younger folks. It was a differentiating idea that also resonated with its target audience. (It's also an idea that never should have been dropped.)

When Seconds Die

Pepsi-Cola found a different way. Those that don't rarely survive.

Advil was the first over-the-counter ibuprofen. Until it came along, there was only Motrin, which was sold only by prescription. In fact, Advil introduced itself as "the same as the prescription drug Motrin." To the prospect that meant serious medicine without the serious price.

The second brand into the category was Nuprin. The third was Medipren. But these brands never found a way to differentiate themselves from Advil. The result is that they died.

Today, only Motrin IB survives with less than a third of Advil's business. The reason they made it, where others didn't, was that they were the first ibuprofen.

The Generic Advantage

One reason the first brand tends to maintain its leadership is that the name often becomes generic. Xerox, the first plain-paper copier, became the name for all plain-paper copiers. People will stand in front of a Ricoh or a Sharp or a Kodak machine and say, "How do I make a Xerox copy?" They will ask for the Kleenex when the box clearly says Scott. They will offer you a Coke when all they have is Pepsi.

How many people ask for cellophane tape instead of Scotch tape? Not many. Most people use brand names when they become generic: Band-Aid, Fiberglas, Formica, Gore-Tex, Jell-O, Krazy Glue, Q-tips, Saran Wrap, and Velcro—to name a few. Some people will go to great lengths to turn a brand name into a generic. "FedEx this package to the coast." If you're introducing the first brand in a new category, you should always try to select a name that can work generically. (Lawyers advise the opposite, but what do they know about marketing?)

Now the Bad News

First or new big ideas can start very slowly and take a long time before commercial acceptance:

- The 35-mm camera took a long time between its first appearance in the 1920s and the Japanese success in the 1960s (forty years).
- Microwave ovens were discovered in 1946, but it was not until the mid-1970s that they gained acceptance (thirty years).

- VCRs were introduced in 1956, but it wasn't until 1975 that the home market took off (twenty years).

- Telephone answering machines evolved slowly in the late 1950s. Demand exploded in the mid-1980s (twenty-five years).

- Video games started in 1972 when the market boomed then went bust. Not until 1985, when Nintendo entered, did demand materialize for the long term (thirteen years).

- Light beer languished while the pioneers spent nearly a decade trying to figure out how to position the product to consumers (nine years).

The moral here is that you have to be prepared to hang in there when you're first and not let someone steal your idea.

Still More Bad News

Being first, even if you hang around for a while, is still no guarantee of success. Consider the stories of imitators that surpassed the pioneers:

- Leica was the technology and market leader for decades in 35-mm cameras until the Japanese copied German technology, improved upon it, and lowered prices. The pioneer failed to react and ended up a bit player.

- Reynolds and Eversharp were the pioneers in ballpoint pens when the fad first ended in the late 1940s. Bic entered last and sold pens as cheap disposables. The pioneers are out of the game.

- Digital Research pioneered CP/M operating systems for personal computers. They were the early standard but did not upgrade for the IBM PC. Microsoft bought an imitative upgrade and became the new standard. Windows arrived and the rest is history.

- Diners Club pioneered the credit card in 1950. They were undercapitalized in a business where money is the key resource. Visa is now everywhere. Diners Club is nowhere.
- de Havilland was a British aircraft maker that rushed to the market with a jet that crashed frequently. Boeing followed with safer, larger, and more powerful jets that didn't crash. Guess who won?
- Sunshine Biscuits introduced Hydrox and pioneered the chocolate sandwich cookie market. National Biscuit (Nabisco) launched Oreo cookies in 1912. Superiority in distribution and advertising resulted in no contest. It became an American original even though there was nothing original about it.

The list of losers goes on, but you get the point. Being first is one thing. Staying first is another. It takes enormous effort and energy to ride that wave. Gillette pioneered razor blades and, to this day, is the dominant leader. They did it with endless innovations and relentless knocking off of anyone who entered the market with a new idea (such as Wilkinson with stainless). Today Gillette has 65 percent of the world's blade business. No one is going to take their business.

Needed: A Good Idea

Successful firsts aren't tricky. They tend to be good ideas. Conversely, unsuccessful firsts tend to be bad ideas.

R.J. Reynolds spent a fortune on the first smokeless cigarette. This is the antithesis of common sense. Their theory was that smokeless cigarettes would appeal to nonsmokers. Unfortunately, nonsmokers don't buy cigarettes.

Something like $325 million went up in smoke (or nonsmoke) with the dismal launch of Premier cigarettes. The cigarettes were hard to light, did not generate any ash (which smokers love to tap and flick), and smelled bad. Reynolds's own president was quoted as saying they "tasted like crap." Premier may have been a first, but it was just plain stupid.

And then we come to Frosty Paws, the first ice cream for dogs. "It's not ice cream, but your dog will think it is," said the introductory ad. Reality check, please. It's pretty well established that Fido will eat almost anything you throw on the floor. Does he need premium-priced fake ice cream? More to the point, are you really going to buy it for him?

Being first with a stupid idea is just, well, stupid. It won't get you anywhere.

One More Sad Tale

So, while being first with an idea is paramount if possible, it has to be a workable differentiating idea. Consider the sad saga of Rosen Motors, which was founded in 1993 and closed in 1997.

The Rosen brothers were impressive people. Harold was a former Hughes Electronics engineer who pioneered the geostationary communications satellite. Ben was the chairman of Compaq Computer and a legend in the personal computer industry.

They poured $24 million and three years into developing an automobile drivetrain with an energy-storing flywheel. This system stored energy that's normally dissipated during braking and released it for sudden bursts of acceleration that a turbine alone couldn't provide. Nice idea in a test vehicle. Bad idea in Detroit, which is not disposed to contract out the guts of its cars to another manufacturer.

The major automakers snubbed Rosen Motors' visionary drivetrain because they had other ideas and flywheel technology didn't figure into their plans. They got squeezed out with what just wasn't a workable differentiating idea. It was just wishful thinking.

A "First" Ignored

A trip into the Yellow Pages to find someone to air-condition your home will turn up the likes of Trane, Fedders, Carrier, and other companies that claim to be able to do the job. If you look at their slogans, you'll see things like "Relax, it's Rheem," "Lennox. One less thing to worry about," "custom-made indoor weather," or "customizing your environment." Finding a difference is hard to do. Could they truly be all the same? Your only choice is to go next door and find out who did your neighbor's home.

But if you really start to do some digging about air conditioning, you'll find out that it all was invented by a gentleman in 1902. Few people know the name of the man responsible for their comfort. He never became famous because he spent most of his time in the laboratory improving on his invention. His name was Willis Carrier.

The opportunity is there for Carrier to use their heritage and reinvent the air conditioner with some new designs.

Instead of presenting themselves as "We're the inside guys," they should stop ignoring their past and set themselves apart by saying, "We're the guys that invented air conditioning."

A Healthy First

Here's a new product "first" we think has a chance to buck the odds.

It's called Airborne, and it's the first health product created to fight airborne germs and viruses. Airborne is a vitamin-herb combination that promises to protect frequent fliers from the unhealthy air at 35,000 feet.

The U.S. dietary supplement market already rings up $14 billion in sales. This new tablet, sold in airport stores, plays to the fears fanned by media reports: Travelers are breathing everybody else's germs in the crowded environment of an airplane cabin.

And the herd effect may give Airborne a lift. Hollywood celebrities like it, and the San Francisco 49ers' training staff swear by it.

A Merger Tale

An organization called Kranson Industries was acquiring a number of organizations that were packaging distributors. These were companies that didn't manufacture packaging but supplied a wide variety of packaging solutions to companies that didn't need a zillion packages per year.

In a short time they were twice as big as the second largest distributor and five times as big as most other distributors. They were ready to become something different.

Kranson put together their two biggest distributors, Tricor and Braun, and became TricorBraun, "the industry's first super distributor."

This new very large organization had the credentials to supply more buying leverage, more design and development support, and more knowledge to solve complex packaging problems.

They introduced this new entity at a big industry trade show, and as CEO Richard Glassman reported, "We blew our lesser competitors away."

Be first and you will automatically be different. If you can hang in there and fight off the imitators, you will be very successful.

First into the Garden

A crowd of smart folks in Austin, Texas, founded Garden.com, the first Internet company to address America's most popular hobby.

Surprisingly, that hobby is gardening, a $46 billion industry. (That's twice the size of the book industry, which e-commerce darling Amazon.com is trying to dominate.)

Gardening is a highly fragmented business. It's regional, tied to climate and soil. But gardeners are passionate and generally affluent. And nobody appears to have more than 1 percent of the market.

Among a batch of cash-sucking e-commerce schemes, Garden.com stands out. It has already signed up 500,000 members. Its Web site sells 16,000 items. The average visitor lingers for half an hour.

The company raised $51 million privately. Now, an IPO for Garden.com is expected to yield another $50 million. Like we said, it's good to be first.

A Do-Good First

There are 500 or so bottled waters out there from giants to pygmies. (More on water in Chapter 11.) So here comes a brand called Keeper Springs Mountain Spring Water that really has an interesting difference: no profit.

Keeper Springs is the product of Tear of the Clouds L.L.C., an environmental group out to raise money for their cause of cleaning up polluted waterways.

Their differentiating idea is on every bottle: All their profits go to the environment. They introduced this product with a wonderful concept: "After just one sip, you've done more for the environment than most politicians."

As the president of their advertising agency says, "We feel we have a very clear point of difference and we should push that difference."[2]

Well said. Giving away all your profits to do good sure is a unique selling proposition. It's also one that sure won't attract many imitators.

A Borrowed First

Being first in one part of the world doesn't preclude someone from borrowing that idea and launching a "first" in his or her own part of the world.

Such is the case for a gentleman in Spain.

Fernandez Pujals, who was raised in Fort Lauderdale, Florida, wasn't shy about borrowing Domino's home delivery idea. He came up with a great name, TelePizza, and with $80,000 became the first home delivery pizza in Madrid.

In a little more than ten years, TelePizza has opened almost 600 stores in half a dozen countries. His "borrowed first" now has a value of $1.85 billion.

As Thomas Edison advised, "Make it a habit to keep on the lookout for novel and interesting ideas that others have used successfully."

In other words, being first often just means being observant.

Attribute Ownership
Is a Way
to Differentiate

The word *attribute* is one of those marketing words that is used widely but not really understood. So let's get our definitions straight before we plunge on.

First, an attribute is a characteristic, peculiarity, or distinctive feature of a person or thing.

Next, persons or things are a mixture of attributes. Each person is different in terms of sex, size, intelligence, skills, and attractiveness. Each product, depending on the category, also has a set of different attributes. Each toothpaste, for example, is different from

95

other toothpastes in terms of cavity prevention, plaque prevention, taste, teeth whitening, and breath protection.

Owning an Attribute

What makes a person or product unique is being known for one of these attributes. Marilyn Monroe was known for her attractiveness. Crest toothpaste is known for its cavity prevention. Marilyn could have had a high degree of intelligence, but it wasn't important. What made her special was that pinup beauty. The same with Crest, as it's all about fighting cavities. What it tasted like wasn't important.

Attribute ownership is probably the number one way to differentiate a product or service.

But beware, you can't own the same attribute or position that your competitor owns. You must seek out another attribute.

Too often a company attempts to emulate the leader: "They must know what works," goes the rationale, "so let's do something similar." Not good thinking.

It's much better to search for an opposite attribute that will allow you to play off against the leader: The key word here is *opposite*—similar won't do.

Coca-Cola was the original and thus the choice of older people. Pepsi successfully positioned itself as the choice of the younger generation.

The world of bourbon is dominated by the two J's, Jim Beam and Jack Daniel's. So Maker's Mark set out to own an attribute that makes their smaller sales more attractive: "handcrafting our bourbon to produce a smooth, soft taste."

Since Crest owned cavities, other toothpastes avoided cavities and jumped on other attributes like taste, whitening, breath protection, and, more recently, baking soda.

If you're not a leader, then your word has to have a narrow focus. Even more important, however, your word has to be "available" in your category. No one else can have a lock on it.

Focus Is the Key

The most effective attributes are simple and benefit oriented. No matter how complicated the product, no matter how complicated the needs of the market, it's always better to focus on one word or benefit rather than two or three or four, and to stay with it. The distinct difference Pepsi always had from Coke was its youth orientation. The more Pepsi becomes homogenized with slogans like "the joy of cola," the more it loses its point of difference.

Also, there's the halo effect. If you strongly establish one benefit, the prospect is likely to give you a lot of other benefits, too. A "thicker" spaghetti sauce implies quality, nourishing ingredients, value, and so on. A "safer" car implies better design and engineering.

Whether the result of a deliberate program or not, most successful companies (or brands) are the ones that "own a word" in the mind of the prospect.

The following sections take you through some of these word or attribute battles in the marketplace.

Attributes Are Not Created Equal

Some attributes are more important to customers than others. You must try to own the most important attribute.

Cavity prevention is the most important attribute in toothpaste. It's the one to own. But what we call the law of exclusivity points to the simple truth that once an attribute is successfully taken by your competition, it's gone. You must move on to a lesser attribute and live with a smaller share of the category. Your job is to seize a different attribute, dramatize the value of your attribute, and thus increase your share.

Such was the case in the automotive field when, some years ago, Detroit was invaded first from Germany and then from Japan with a new attribute.

Attributes in Automobiles

For years, Detroit dominated the world of automobiles with its attributes of "big," "powerful," and "comfortable."

Then along came Volkswagen with the first "small" car that was "economical," "reliable," and "ugly." Detroit laughed and said to themselves, "America wants big, good-looking cars. And we have the research to prove it."

Then came the Japanese with their small but better-looking cars. Detroit wasn't laughing anymore as 1,348,046 small cars were sold in 1997. Forty percent of that total went to the Japanese and Germans.

If you study the automotive category, you'll find that the strongest brands own important attributes:

BMW	driving
Volvo	safety
Mercedes	engineering
Jaguar	styling
Toyota and Honda	reliability
Ferrari	speed

Brands such as Chevrolet, Nissan, Mercury, and Oldsmobile are weak brands because they are unfocused and they don't own an attribute.

No Attribute Uncovered

Gillette never laughs at new attributes that are the opposite of their current products. The dominance of the world's number one razor blade maker revolves around its high-tech razors and cartridge systems. When an upstart from France brought an opposite attribute to the category in the form of a "disposable" razor, Gillette could have laughed and wheeled out its research on how America wants hefty, expensive, high-tech razors. But it didn't.

Instead, Gillette jumped in with a disposable razor of its own, called Good News. By spending heavily, Gillette was able to win the battle of the disposables.

Today the Gillette Good News razor dominates the disposable category, which has grown to dominate the razor blade business. Moral: You can't predict the size of a new attribute's share, so never laugh.

Attributes in Credit Cards

Visa has dominated the credit card world by taking possession of the attribute of being "everywhere." They now account for nearly 53 percent of the $1.16 trillion in annual credit card transactions. This is up from 44 percent in 1985. That same year they were almost even with MasterCard. Today they enjoy a 2 to 1 ratio over the other bankcard.

MasterCard's problem is that they don't own an attribute of their own. They are trying to act like Visa. (Big mistake.) If Visa is "everywhere" in those glorious world traveler commercials, MasterCard should have focused on the "everyday usage" attribute. They should have become "Main Street's charge card" in places like grocery stores and gas stations. (Ironically, that's what American Express is now pushing.)

Not owning a different attribute has been an expensive lesson for MasterCard.

Attributes in Retailing

There is no tougher battle than in mass merchandising where the big chains are battling it out. Those with differentiating ideas are doing fine. Those without aren't.

The biggest and probably the toughest big chain is Wal-Mart. Their attribute is pretty straightforward: everyday low prices. And they have the muscle and technology to back it up.

Target, the $21 billion dollar division of Dayton Hudson, has gotten away from the dowdy discount image by making low-price shopping hip. Their differentiating attribute could be described as "mass with class." And they have the advertising and nicely designed products to back it up. (Target's devotees like to pronounce the name with a French twist: "tar-zhay.")

Ames is a regional $4-billion-in-sales operation that has survived nicely by targeting a clientele below the Wal-Mart set. One could describe their differentiating attribute as "mass with no class." To support that concept they cut costs and stock up to sell to working people, old people, and big people. They're heavy in textured acrylic.

Caldor was a large 140-store chain in the Northeast. They had no differentiating attribute. They died and were buried at the beginning of 1999.

As we said on the cover of this book, differentiate or die.

Attributes in Fast Food

Burger King was unsuccessful when it tried to take the attribute "fast" from McDonald's. What should Burger King have done? Use the opposite attribute? The exact opposite attribute, "slow," won't do for a fast-food place (although there is an element of slowness in Burger King's "have it your way" concept).

A single trip to any McDonald's should be enough to find another attribute that McDonald's owns: "kids." This is indeed the place to which kids drag their parents, and McDonald's has the swing sets to prove it. This sets up an opportunity vividly demonstrated by the Coke and Pepsi battle. If McDonald's owns kids, then Burger King has the opportunity to position itself for the older crowd, which includes any kid who doesn't want to be perceived as a kid. That generally works out to be everyone over the age of ten. (Not a bad market.)

To make the concept work, Burger King would have to sacrifice and give all the little kids to McDonald's. While this might mean getting rid of a few swing sets, it allows Burger King to hang "kiddieland" on McDonald's (see Chapter 20 on sacrifice).

To drive the concept into prospects' minds, Burger King would need a term. It could be "grow up." Grow up to the flame-broiled taste of Burger King.

Attributes in Water

Even a commodity product such as water can be differentiated by an attribute. While water as a product could be considered boring, it sure is a hot commodity in the marketplace. In the United States, bulk sales of water are over 3 billion gallons. (Carbonated soft drinks are 14.6 billion gallons.)

To marketers, liquid gold comes in bottles as people are paying money for nothing but water. So it's not surprising to see water fights breaking out all over the world. In Belgium, for example, you have the story of Bru, a lightly sparkling mineral water located in the Ardennes.

To be specific, the source is Stoumont, in the AmbeEve Valley in the Ardennes, a protected region.

Light Bubbles in Belgium

Since Bru was only lightly sparkling, it was caught midway between flat and full-bodied sparkling waters. Thus it lacked character.

When you have a lemon, you make lemonade.

The company introduced the attribute of "light bubbles," which they called "pearls" or *l'eau perlée*. Sales went from 1 million liters in 1981 to 42 million in 1996. Bru, with its attribute difference of light bubbles, is now the top-selling sparkling water in Belgium.

Low Sodium in Argentina

In Argentina, the number one bottled water is Villavicencio, a mountain spring water with about 30 percent of the market. The other mountain water is ECO de los Andes with a 10 percent share.

For ECO to make any progress, they have to find a way to differentiate themselves from the leader, thus supplying a reason to prefer their brand. A quick look at the labels identifies that difference. Villavicencio, because of where they are bottling their water, has a very high sodium content (272 milligrams per 1.5-liter bottle) as compared to ECO's content (10.4 milligrams per 1.5-liter bottle). Interestingly, ECO's sodium content lines up perfectly with the American Heart Association's recommended sodium intake.

ECO's low sodium attribute has enabled them to position themselves as "the low-sodium mountain water." Now they have a unique selling proposition that makes them not only healthier but also different. (Rosser Reeves would have approved.)

The Use of "Negative" Attributes

Hanging "Kiddieland" on McDonald's or "high sodium" on Villavicencio is an example of attaching a negative attribute to your competitor.

This can be a very effective way to set up your attribute. We call this repositioning the competition.

Scope did this by hanging "bad taste" on Listerine en route to becoming the "good-tasting" mouthwash. (That was easy.)

BMW did it to Mercedes Benz when they set up the following comparison:

> The ultimate sitting machine
> versus the ultimate driving machine.

By repositioning Mercedes as a living room on wheels, they very quickly were able to lay claim to the attribute of drivability.

If you can hang a negative on your competition en route to setting up what makes you different, you have a program that will be twice as effective.

Bloodless in New Jersey

There are times when you have to create an attribute.

Such was the case of the Englewood (New Jersey) Hospital and Medical Center, which found a way to differentiate themselves from the eighty-two hospitals in the tristate area around New York. They created an attribute called "bloodless surgery."

It all began with an effort to serve the Jehovah's Witness population that refuses blood transfusions because of their religious beliefs. Once the techniques and procedures were in place, promoting this attribute not only attracted their target Jehovah's Witness segment but the broader general population as well. (Who wants to lose blood?)

Pioneering and taking ownership of the attribute of "bloodless medicine and surgery" resulted in a powerful differentiating idea. Patients from twenty-two states and ten countries have traveled to Englewood for what they see as a big difference in the way surgery is performed.

Bigger in Massachusetts

When it comes to museums, you don't always think of bigger as being a better attribute. After all, it can take days to wander through the confusing corridors of some museums.

But with contemporary art, size does matter. These creations can be enormous. The title of a 1981 work by Robert Rauschenberg is not an exaggeration: *The ¼ Mile or 2 Furlong Piece.* Most galleries couldn't even dream of exhibiting this monster.

Enter the Massachusetts Museum of Contemporary Art in the Berkshire town of North Adams. With one gallery the size of a football field and another with a soaring 40-foot ceiling, Mass MoCA (its nickname) proudly differentiates itself as the largest center for visual and performing arts in the United States. (It may be the largest in the world.)

Where did all this space come from? The museum is housed in a vast, abandoned nineteenth-century factory complex that sprawls over thirteen acres. To date, six buildings have been transformed into 250,000 square feet of galleries and theater space.

Simple in Massachusetts

There are times when you can take advantage of the environment in a category en route to owning an attribute.

Such is the case in this high-tech, networked world where companies are trying to set up intranets for their own organization or between themselves and their customers. To do this is a complex piece of work using outside experts and a great deal of money.

A company called IntraNetics came up with a piece of software that enabled a company to quickly install a suite of essential applications that could be easily modified and connected to customers and partners.

They were able to claim: "Finally. A simple way to build a powerful intranet." In a complex world, it always works if you can preempt the attribute of being simple.

Is "Being Green" a Difference?

Finally, how about the environment itself?

In these environmentally sensitive times, many are looking at "being green" as an attribute that they hope will make them different. But the jury is still out on this. The debate has become polarized.

A group of business academics assert that it pays to be green. They argue that firms can increase profits if they set ambitious environmental targets. A second group of executives and academics emphasize that firms exist to serve their shareholders and serving the environment is not very realistic.

Well, let us give you some guidelines on being environmentally sensitive as a differentiating attribute. In order to make a strategy of environmental product differentiation succeed, a business must satisfy three requirements:

1. The business must find, or create, a willingness among customers to pay for environmental quality.
2. The business must establish credible information about the environmental attributes of its products.
3. Its innovation must be defensible against imitation by competitors.

In other words, you've got your work cut out for you. Our view is that, at present, companies should be good citizens but find another way to differentiate themselves.

Leadership Is a Way to Differentiate

Leadership is the most powerful way to differentiate a brand. The reason is that it's the most direct way to establish the credentials of a brand. And credentials are the collateral you put up to guarantee the performance of your brand.

Also, when you have leadership credentials, your prospect is likely to believe almost anything you say about your brand. (Because you're the leader.)

Leadership Psychology

Humans tend to equate "bigness" with success, status, and leadership. We give respect and admiration to the biggest.

In their book *Mindwatching: Why People Behave The Way They Do*, psychologists Hans and Michael Eysenck reported on a famous study.[1]

A man named "Mr. England" was introduced to a number of classes of college students in America. He was referred to as either "Mr. England, a student from Cambridge" or "Professor England from Cambridge."

Afterward, the students were asked to estimate the man's height. As Mr. England climbed in status from student to professor, he gained 5 inches in the eyes of the students.

Bigness also pays off in dollars and cents. A survey of male graduates of the University of Pittsburgh revealed that the tallest students (6 feet 2 inches and over) received an average starting salary at least 12 percent higher than those who were under 6 feet.

So it is in the world of business, where height is measured by sales or market share.

Owning a Category

Powerful leaders can take ownership of the word that stands for the category. You can test the validity of a leadership claim by a word association test.

If the given words are *computer, copier, chocolate bar,* and *cola,* the four most associated words are *IBM, Xerox, Hershey's,* and *Coke.*

An astute leader will go one step further to solidify its position. Heinz owns the word *ketchup.* But Heinz went on to isolate the most important ketchup attribute. "Slowest ketchup in the West" is how the company is preempting the thickness attribute. Owning the word *slow* helps Heinz maintain a 50 percent market share.

Don't Be Afraid to Brag

Despite all of the foregoing points about the power of being the perceived leader, we continue to come across leaders who don't want to talk about their leadership. Their response about avoiding this claim to what is rightfully theirs is often the same: We don't want to brag.

Well, a leader who doesn't brag is the best thing that can happen to its competition. When you've clawed your way to the top of the mountain, you had better plant your flag and take some pictures.

And besides, you can often find a nice way to express your leadership. One of our favorite leadership slogans does just that: "Fidelity Investments. Where 12 million investors put their trust."

If you don't take credit for your achievement, the one right behind you will find a way to claim what is rightfully yours.

If you doubt this, consider the following saga.

Two Leaders from Brazil

For years, the two big beers in Brazil were Antarctica and Brahma. Antarctica was number one and Brahma was a close-behind number two.

Then Brahma started an advertising campaign claiming leadership (a *cerveja* number one). They added point-of-sale hands with the index finger symbolizing number one. But here's the surprise. When they started this, Antarctica was still the leader but no one knew it because they had not planted their flag of leadership.

When the dust settled, guess who moved into first place? You're right. Brahma is now number one. The reason: When people thought that they weren't drinking the leading beer, they quickly shifted to Brahma and what started out as an untruth became the truth.

The moral: While people love underdogs, they buy the overdogs.

But there is a happy ending to this story, as Antarctica and Brahma have now merged their companies. They can now say they both are number one.

Our Kind of Leader

Hertz is not shy about being the leader. They are a classic example of how to keep a market leadership story fresh and meaningful over the years.

Today the message is "Hertz, and not exactly." Says Brian Kennedy, Hertz's executive vice president of marketing and sales, "The underlying premise of the 'Not exactly' ads is to distinguish us from the competition."[2]

This is the latest in a long line of different ways that Hertz has expressed its leadership. At the dawn of the car rental business, it was people flying though the air and "Let Hertz put you in the driver's seat."

With the company clearly established as number one, they got busy adding services: "The biggest should do more. It's only right."

By 1975, O.J. Simpson started racing through airports. He was "the superstar in rent-a-car." So was Hertz.

Later variations of that idea included "the number one way to rent a car" and "where winners rent."

As Hertz took aim at vacation travelers as well as the business renter, the theme evolved into "number one for everyone" and "America's wheels."

Pretty monotonous, huh? Decades of selling America an idea it loves: leadership.

So monotonous that today Hertz has U.S. revenues of $2.3 billion, a fleet of 500,000 vehicles in 140 countries, and a market share of 30 percent.

Who's the world's largest car rental company? Exactly.

Different Forms of Leadership

Leadership comes in many flavors, any of which can be an effective way to differentiate yourself. Here's a quick sampling of different ways to leadership:

- *Sales leadership.* The most often used strategy by leaders is pronouncing how well they sell. The Toyota Camry is the best-selling car in America. But others can claim their own sales leadership by carefully counting in different ways. Lincoln is the top-selling luxury car. Chrysler's Dodge Caravan is the top-selling minivan. The Ford Explorer is the top sport utility vehicle. This approach works because people tend to buy what others buy.

- *Technology leadership.* Some companies with long histories of technological breakthroughs can use this form of leadership as a differentiator. In Austria, a rayon fiber manufacturer called Lenzing isn't the sales leader but they are the "world's leader in viscose fiber technology." They pioneered many of the industry breakthroughs in new and improved rayon. In Cincinnati, a machinery manufacturer called Milacron is one of the "world's leaders in manufacturing technology." They have the widest array of plastic machines and cutting tool technologies. This type of leadership works because people are impressed with companies that develop new technologies. (They figure they know more.)

- *Performance leadership.* Companies have products that aren't big sellers but are big performers. This can also be used as a way to separate yourself from your lesser performing competition. Silicon Graphics is such a company. They use Cray supercomputers, visual workstations that make those Hollywood special effects possible, and high-powered wideband servers that do graphics and data better than most. As the result, they are the "world's leader in high performance computing." This would work because companies with money often want the best, even if they don't need it.

Leadership Is a Platform

Leadership is a wonderful platform from which to tell the story of how you got to be number one. As we said earlier, people will believe whatever you say if they perceive you as a leader.

Consider the story of Dreyer's Grand ice cream. This is a company that has two brands: Dreyer's, which is west of the Rockies, and Edy's, which is east of the Rockies. (They were named after their two founders, William Dreyer and Joseph Edy.)

These two brands have made the company America's leading ice cream maker, which is their sales leadership differentiating idea.

But what also makes them unique, and in great measure what has made them number one, is their direct delivery to stores. Unlike their major competitors, they own a fleet of refrigerated trucks manned by experts who deliver and place the ice cream in retail stores. This process bypasses the usual distributor freezers, and thus ensures a fresher product. (Freezers are the natural enemy of ice cream.) Their philosophy: It takes great care to make a great ice cream.

Their leadership story, coupled with their direct delivery story, makes a compelling and logical argument as to why they make "America's favorite ice cream."

The Strength of Leadership

What makes a company strong is not the product or the service. It's the position it owns in the mind. The strength of Hertz is in its leadership position, not the quality of its rent-a-car service. It's easier to stay on top than to get there.

Can you name a company that has overturned a leader? Crest did it in toothpaste, thanks to the American Dental Association's seal of approval. (Ironically, Colgate has regained the lead with its germ-killing Total toothpaste.) Duracell did it in batteries, thanks to "alkaline." Budweiser did it in beer, and Marlboro did it in cigarettes. But it rarely happens.

A survey of twenty-five leading brands from the year 1923 proves this point. Today, twenty-one of those brands are still in first place. Three are in second place, and one is in fifth place.

Even changes in rank don't happen very often. If marketing were a horse race, it would be a deadly dull affair. In the fifty-six years since World War II, there has been only one change in position in the top three U.S. automobile companies.

In 1950, Ford Motor Company moved past Chrysler Corporation into second place. Since then the order has been General Motors, Ford, and Chrysler all the way. Monotonous, isn't it?

The "stickiness" of a marketing race, the tendency for companies or brands to remain in the same position year after year, also underscores the importance of securing a good position in the first place. Improving your position might be difficult, but once you do, it becomes relatively easy to maintain that new position.

When you do get on top, make sure the marketplace knows it. Too many companies take their leadership for granted and never exploit it. All this does is keep the door open for competition. If you get the chance, slam the door in your competition's face.

The Leading Lollipop?

Every category has a leader, but not every leader is known. Consider the lowly lollipop. You've seen them all your life, but if we asked you who makes the best-selling lollipop in the world, you probably wouldn't have a clue.

Now, if we told you that one lollipop company sells twice as much as its closest competitor, you'd be a little impressed. The fact that this company sells its lollipops in 170 countries would impress you a little more. The fact that they produce over 20 million lollipops a day and their yearly production will circle the globe twelve times will impress you a lot more.

And when we finally tell you about their popularity with young and old kids alike, you probably will say to yourself, "They must make one hell of a lollipop. I should try one."

The name of the one to try is Chupa Chups, the world's favorite lollipop. You'll find them in Barcelona, Spain.

See what a difference a little leadership can make?

Heritage Is a Differentiating Idea

In Chapter 9 we discussed the fact that minds are insecure. And any strategy that helps people overcome their insecurities is a good one.

Heritage has the power to make your product stand out. It can be a powerful differentiating idea because there appears to be a natural psychological importance in having a long history, one that makes people secure in their choice.

When we started to study why this is so, we assumed that being around a long time suggested that a company knew what they were doing. People figured that they must have been doing something right.

But unlike countries such as China and Japan, where elders are given the utmost respect, our culture tends to have an abhorrence of old age. Everybody wants to be young. Old and wise means out of it and passé.

The Psychology of Heritage

When we asked Dr. Carol Moog why heritage is meaningful, this consumer psychologist made the following observations:

> The psychological importance of heritage may derive from the power of being a participant in a continuous line that connects and bonds one to the right to be alive, to a history that one carries forward from the living past, through death and on into the next generation. The link is a link to immortality. Without a sense of heritage, of known ancestors, people are vulnerable to feeling isolated, abandoned, emotionally cut off, and ungrounded. Without a line from the past, it is difficult to believe in a line to the future.
>
> The emphasis on heritage, then, is on continuity, on one's defeat of death by remaining part of the flow. Embracing companies and products with this kind of lineage allows people to participate in these powerful links to a continuous life. When traditions are passed down, they are imbued with the life of ancestors. Continuity is incorporated, ingested. People become larger; life goes on. When entities, such as companies, have their heritage swallowed up or obliterated, they literally break a trust bond, abandon people who have counted on that link, generate passivity, and create emotional numbing. Distrust, cynicism, and detachment clearly do not stimulate sales.[1]

There you go, everything you wanted to know about heritage but were afraid to ask.

A Substitute for Leadership

Another way to look at this approach is to recognize that being around a long time also gives prospects the feeling that they are dealing with an industry leader. If not the biggest, they certainly are a leader in longevity.

It's no wonder that marketers display their tradition and culture as a way of telling you why they are different.

As early as 1919, a Steinway piano was described in an advertisement as "the instrument of the immortals."

More recently, Cross trumpeted its pens as "flawless classics,
since 1846."

Sotheby's, the famous auction house, goes one century better by
proclaiming its founding in 1744.

Glenlivet Scotch positions itself as "the father of all Scotch. His
Majesty's Government bestowed on The Glenlivet Distillery the
very first license under The Act of 1823 to distill single malt
whiskey in the Highlands."

Budweiser is proclaiming their beer as "America's classic lager
since 1876." (That sure is a lot better than lizards talking
about frogs.)

Some of these brands are leaders in their category. Some aren't.
But they all sound very impressive and different.

Bringing Heritage Forward

But tradition isn't always enough, says an Associated Press business
writer. "Companies of all stripes have spent recent years devising
new marketing tactics that blend consumer-comforting tradition
with the progressiveness that's crucial to continued success."[2]

Wells Fargo Bank, of Pony Express and stagecoach beginnings,
takes its original idea and makes it relevant by simply stating, "Fast
then. Fast now." The difference is that today's stagecoaches travel
at the speed of light via advanced computer networks.

L.L. Bean jazzes up its catalog, goes online, and introduces
women's clothing—while carefully maintaining its New England
image. Says a company spokesman, "You take the classic appeal and
you take it to another generation."

The continued success of Tabasco in the pepper sauce business is
an example of the balance between honoring your heritage and
looking forward.

Its advertising strikes traditional themes such as down-home
Louisiana bayous and pepper mash aged in oak barrels. But the

company also presents itself as with-it and trendy, with Tabasco neckties, Cajun-cooking festivals, and new Tabasco-laced drinks that originate in rural Louisiana oyster bars.

One popular drink is the prairie fire, which combines a shot of Tequila with a splash of Tabasco.

"There are all sorts of balancing acts needed in marketing," says company president Paul C.P. McIlhenny.

"American history is full of stories of companies that could not adjust to changing markets," says Robert Sobel, a professor emeritus of business history at Hofstra University. "The danger is when the company president says, 'My father came up with this product and it's a monument to his memory and we're not going to get rid of it as long as I'm here.' And of course, he's not there four years later. If you're wedded to the past, you're going to fail."[3]

Heritage in Politics and Law

Consider the instant success of George W. Bush as a candidate for president. He was the "compassionate Conservative" from Texas. Just what is a compassionate Conservative? Well, no one was quite sure.

What they were sure of was that George W. had a presidential heritage. (He even looks like his ex-president father.) He started off with a heritage that made him different from the other candidates.

The law firms of RisCasi & Davis and Trantolo & Trantolo—based in New England—are two strong examples of heritage marketing in this category. Both firms have strong ties to past generations and use those ties effectively to differentiate themselves from the competition. Trantolo & Trantolo has been particularly effective—using advertising that speaks to the "first" Trantolo's immigrant roots and his protection of immigrant families with little power of their own. The law firm's positioning draws on both historical positions—long service to the community and serving the less powerful—using the idea of "fighting for the little guy" as their link to that heritage.

Doubling Back on Heritage

It's never too late to tell your heritage story. Such is the case of Franzia, America's best-selling brand of wine. It's a wine that is sold "on tap" in a 5-liter box. It's also a wine with an amazing and little-known heritage that is just being introduced to America.

Here's the brand-new heritage story that soon will be told:

Teresa Franzia:
The Little Lady That Pioneered America's Wine Business

While just 4′10″ tall, this lady from Italy played a very large role in what has become a very big business.

She arrived in San Francisco in 1900 and settled on a farm in California's Central Valley. She and her family started growing grapes on rich, sandy loam soil that even today, is the best for miles around.

After prohibition was repealed, Teresa made a decision to make wine from her grapes. She borrowed $10,000 from A.P. Giovanni, the founder of Bank of America to begin the winery. She gave half of this loan to her daughter and her husband Ernest Gallo.

The rest is history. With that beginning, she became the pioneer of America's wine business. The Franzia business and that of her son-in-law, Ernest Gallo, today represent over 50 percent of all the wine made in this country.

That story turns an ordinary table wine into a very special table wine with a unique heritage.

The moral: It's never too late to tell your life history. (But only if it's an interesting one.)

DDB Tries to Double Back

DDB Worldwide Communications is a large advertising agency that is the successor agency to Doyle Dane Bernbach, the organization that many claim invented modern advertising. (We discussed Bill Bernbach in Chapter 5.)

Doyle Dane was founded in 1949. DDB capitalized on its fiftieth anniversary as a way to burnish its reputation and stand out from myriad competition.

As reported in *The New York Times*, agency head Keith Reinhard stated, "We're trying to reclaim the Bernbach legacy. The Doyle Dane heritage represents a brand equity we should leverage."

While trying to double back on that heritage is a nice idea, it won't cover up the basic problem that this heritage belongs to a name that's long gone. As one of the creative alumni said in that same article, "A horrible mistake was made when they changed the name after the merger. It was like changing the name of Coca-Cola."[4]

It may be too late, Keith. Bill Bernbach's heritage has been buried with his agency's name.

Updating Heritage

There are times when you have to change to survive. Consider the case of the fabled Greenbrier, the 222-year-old resort hotel in West Virginia.

They are looking to add a casino in hopes of keeping the A-list vacationers coming. The gambling hall will be remodeled after Monte Carlo's lavish Hôtel Hermitage.

The hotel's president, Ted Kleisner, says that the Greenbrier must add the casino to stay competitive or risk ending up "just another *grande dame*."

Locational Heritage

An important aspect of heritage is where you come from.

If you're selling vodka and you come from Russia, you certainly have a nice story to tell.

If you're selling computers and you come from the United States, you have a big advantage.

If you're selling cars and you come from Yugoslavia, you've got problems. (The Yugo was doomed.)

The reason why "where you come from" is so important is that countries can be differentiated by products.

That's because, over the years, countries have become well known for certain products. As a result, the country of origin affords a product a certain set of credentials. If it's from there, it must be good. Or, conversely, if it's from there, it must be bad. Here's a quick list of countries and what they can add to a product in terms of locational heritage:

United States	computers and airplanes
Japan	automobiles and electronics
Germany	engineering and beer
Switzerland	banking and watches
Italy	design and clothing
France	wine and perfume
United Kingdom	royalty and racing cars
Russia	vodka and caviar
Argentina	beef and leather
New Zealand	lamb and kiwis
Australia	Crocodile Dundee

The trick here is to avoid the Yugo trap, or coming from a place that not only doesn't help your efforts, but hurts them.

High-Tech from Argentina?

Such was the case of a high-tech product whose heritage was from a country known for steaks, not semiconductors.

The company is called Multiscan and they make a laser bar-code reading device. In fact, they were on their way to building a leadership position in this type of scanning device.

Our advice was to use their leadership in laser bar-code reading devices as their differentiator. But we questioned whether people would believe that a high-tech leader could be from Argentina. Luckily, the company had an office in the United States, and they were willing to disguise their origin.

Multiscan moved its headquarters from Argentina to the United States. Now they had the right heritage and, to go with it, what has proven to be a very successful high-tech export business.

Anticompetitor Heritage

There are times when you can use your competitors' heritage against them. That was the case many years ago when Stolichnaya ran an ad that said:

> Most American vodkas look Russian.
> Stolichnaya is different. It is Russian.

But when Stolichnaya stopped using its heritage as a differentiator, Absolut took over the lead in high-end vodka. Common sense and history point to the fact that the only strategy that Stolichnaya should pursue is that of heritage.

They should take advantage of a little-known fact: Absolut is made by a Swedish vodka company.

They should reposition Absolut where it belongs, in Sweden, while they take advantage of their own Russian heritage. The advertisement they should run would have the headline:

> Absolut Sweden versus Absolute Russian.

Swedish vodka just doesn't sound as good as Russian vodka. Everyone knows that Russian vodka is the real thing.

And consider the looming battle between Procter & Gamble and Wal-Mart as the giant retailer is launching a private-label laundry soap called Sam's American Choice to compete with Tide.

While Procter & Gamble doesn't seem too concerned about a soap that's priced 25 to 30 percent lower, they might get ready to unleash the news that Wal-Mart's soap is made by Huish Detergents Inc.

Would you trust your wash to a company called Huish? Not likely.

A French Success

L'Oréal is a French cosmetic giant that uses locational heritage in a way that has produced a decade of double-digit growth.

Its secret is to use heritage as a way of conveying the allure of different cultures through its many products. Whether it's selling Italian elegance, New York street smarts, or French beauty through its brands, L'Oréal reaches out to a vast range of people across incomes and cultures.

As *Business Week* magazine reports, "While many companies seek to homogenize their brands to make them palatable in myriad cultures, CEO Owen-Jones has taken L'Oréal's products in the opposite direction. He wants them to embody their country of origin, turning what many marketing gurus consider a narrowing factor into a marketing virtue."[5]

While L'Oréal's Maybelline might be a ho-hum brand in the United States, in Shanghai the fact that it comes from America makes it very trendy. (And very different.)

Family Heritage

In a world that's seeing the big get bigger, an effective way to separate yourself from the striving herd is to stay a family business. While taxes and ensuing generations don't always make this easy, it can be a powerful concept if the family can be held together.

People appear to feel more kindly toward a family-run business as opposed to a cold, impersonal public corporation that's beholden to a bunch of greedy stockholders. Family members can be just as greedy. But, because what goes on is never reported, all that greed is kept behind closed doors.

A family business is also believed to be more involved with their product than with their stock price. They also are given higher marks for community involvement because they tend to be natives of the town where the company was founded. We've also discovered that a family business tends to treat their employees more like family. There's a feeling of having grown up together.

No company exemplifies this more than a billion-dollar family company called Rich's Frozen Foods. Their family ownership is a unique difference. That, coupled with size, makes them a counterpoint to the large, impersonal corporations that make up their main competition.

They dramatized this difference by stating that we "care for our customers like only a family can."

They also make the point that in today's competitive world a family company is in a better position to serve their customers. The simple reasons: They don't have to worry about stockholders, earnings, and Wall Street. All their energies go into their products.

Now that is a very nice, logical argument explaining why their family heritage makes them not only different but better.

A Heritage Landmark

A local family retail business can become an important part of a community. Such is the story of the Troast Vision & Hearing Center in Ridgewood, New Jersey, a suburb of New York City.

The family patriarch, Robert C. Troast, a former National Optician of the Year, explains it this way: "When I started the business, I never dreamed it would become a family business. My main concern was to provide quality care to my neighbors. Now, 47 years later, we're practically a landmark. There's something special about being part of a community. A lot of my patients and I go way back. Many times when someone new walks in, I already know the parents, the aunts and uncles, the cousins. In some cases, our kids grew up together and now I'm seeing the grandchildren."

Speaking of kids, his son Ron and daughter-in-law Karen now run the family business. They're active in the Chamber of Commerce, in the church, in the Little League.

All of which sure makes them very different. And they're doing nicely, thank you, in the shadow of the superstores in the nearby malls.

The Character

An interesting way to exploit a brand's heritage is with the character that made the brand famous in the first place.

The Jolly Green Giant. Colonel Sanders for Kentucky Fried Chicken. Charlie the tuna for Star-Kist. The characters make these brands different.

It's no wonder that many of these personalities are being dusted off and returned to duty. The Jolly Green Giant has been awakened and is back pushing canned and frozen vegetables. And Planters' Mr. Peanut has returned as a dignified pitchman with a link to the past.

As David Yale, the general manager of Planters, reported in *The New York Times*, "The character has become a leverage point to talk about the quality, the taste and fun that separates us from other nuts."[6]

A schoolboy created Mr. Peanut in 1916. Bringing him back capitalizes on nostalgia among older shoppers and the trend for "retro chic" styles among the young.

Everything old is not only new again, but different.

Market Specialty Is a Differentiating Idea

People are impressed with those who concentrate on a specific activity or product. They perceive them as experts. And as experts, they tend to give them more knowledge and experience then they sometimes deserve. This isn't surprising when you consider the definition of *expert:* "one having much training and knowledge in some special field."

Conversely, the generalist is rarely given expertise in many fields of endeavor no matter how good he or she may be. Common sense tells the prospect that a single person or company cannot be expert in everything.

A Lesson Learned

Many years ago at General Electric we learned the power of the specialist over the generalist.

At the time, GE was launching a concept called the "turnkey power plant." The concept was simple. General Electric would go to an electric utility with their ability to put all the pieces together. At the end of the process, they would give the utility the keys to the completed plant. (A one-stop shopping concept.)

Nice idea, right? Wrong.

The utility said, "Thank you very much. We'll give you the turbine generators; other specialists will get the controls, switch gear, et cetera."

Even though it was General Electric, the inventor of electricity, the utilities wanted the best of the breed: the specialists.

Another Lesson Learned

Well, GE figured, those utility guys think they know everything. Let's go to the lady of the house and offer her a "GE kitchen."

It was no different. The lady of the house said, "Thank you very much. We'll give you the refrigerator; KitchenAid gets the dishwasher, Maytag the washing machine, et cetera."

Even though it was General Electric, the big kahuna in appliances, the lady of the house wanted the best of the breed: the specialists.

Big Names Are Weak

Generalists like General Electric, though their names are big, are weak in the market.

Consider a big food name like Kraft. When that name is taken out against specialist brand names, nothing good happens. In mayonnaise, Hellmann's trounces them. In jellies, Smuckers kills them. In mustard, French's annihilates them. In yogurt, Dannon destroys them.

Lucky for Kraft they have some specialist brands of their own. In fact, Kraft's biggest brand is one that few people recognize as a Kraft product. It's Philadelphia brand cream cheese. Even though "Kraft" is on the package, people don't even see it. To most, it's all about those little cheesemakers in Philadelphia.

The Same Goes for Retail

Take the retail industry. Which retailers are in trouble today? The department stores. And what's a department store? A place that sells everything. That's a recipe for disaster because it's very hard to differentiate an "everything" place.

Campeau, L.J. Hooker, and Gimbel's all wound up in bankruptcy court. Hills department stores filed for bankruptcy. Macy's, the worlds' largest store, filed for bankruptcy. While some department stores have emerged intact, it indicates how tough the world is becoming for this kind of store.

Interstate Department Stores also went bankrupt. So the company looked at the books and decided to focus on the only product it made money on: toys. As long as Interstate was going to focus on toys, it decided to change its name to Toys "R" Us. Today Toys "R" Us does 20 percent of the retail toy business in the country.

As we wrote earlier, many retail chains are successfully patterning themselves on the Toys "R" Us formula: a narrow focus with in-depth stock. Staples and Blockbuster Video are examples.

In the retail field generally, the big successes are the specialists:

- *The Limited.* Upscale clothing for working women.
- *The Gap.* Casual clothing for the young at heart.
- *Benetton.* Wool and cotton clothing for young swingers.
- *Victoria's Secret.* Sexy undergarments.
- *Foot Locker.* Athletic shoes.
- *Banana Republic.* Upmarket casual wear.

(When a clothing chain with a name like Banana Republic can be successful, you know we live in the age of the specialist.)

The Specialist Has Weapons

Since differentiation takes place in the mind, specialists have weapons they can use to pre-empt their specialty in the mind.

They can focus on one product, one benefit, and one message. Such was the case in the battery business when Duracell focused on alkaline batteries only. Eveready, the generalist, had this type of battery in their lineup but they didn't specialize.

Duracell grabbed a brilliant name, preempted the "long-lasting" attribute, and ran off with their business. Even Eveready's Energizer bunny couldn't slow down the specialist, who now is the leader with 45 percent of the business. (In the latest numbers, even third-place Ray-O-Vac is making gains on the bunny.)

Becoming the Expert

The specialist has a chance to nail down an expertise as a differentiator.

In the business of environmental consulting, there are a lot of players, big and small, all of whom are doing pretty much the same thing. A company in Boston called ENSR has come up with a unique expertise: environmental due diligence.

In other words, when an international real estate or business transaction takes place, this company offers to use its global resources to evaluate the environmental aspects of the deal. That specialty not only differentiates them from their competitors, but sets them up to come back and solve the problems their work has uncovered.

A Publisher's Dream

Unless you're an automobile buff, you've probably never heard of a monthly magazine called *Hemmings Motor News*. But this may be the ultimate specialist success in publishing, where expertise in a given field is the holy grail.

Hemmings sells 265,000 copies a month. It grosses $20 million a year. A typical issue runs 800 pages and is crammed with 20,000 advertisements, offering everything from a wheel bearing set for a Model T Ford (yours for $55) to a 1932 Rolls-Royce Henley roadster (a steal at $650,000).

The bulk of the magazine consists of small black-and-white classified ads, prepaid by check or credit card. The editorial content is miniscule. The sales department is miniscule.

Terry Ehrich, the owner of one of publishing's great cash cows, says the magazine has ridden the popularity of car collecting and car restoring.

"I'm just a mediocre jockey on a helluva horse," he says.[1] A horse that happens to be a helluva specialist idea.

Becoming Generic

The ultimate weapon for a specialist, as discussed earlier, is to become generic. This is where your brand name represents the product as well as the category.

Gatorade is a very powerful specialist that has reached that level in sports drinks.

While it's not easy to become a Xerox in copiers or a Scotch in tapes, the specialist has a chance to hit what is the highest level in brand success.

Now the Bad News

A successful specialist has to stay specialized. You can't begin to chase other business, because you'll begin to erode your perceptions of being a specialist. (More on this in Chapter 19.)

Heart surgeons know this instinctively. They don't decide to go after knee replacements just because they've become big business.

Most marketers don't like to be locked into one business or specialty. They want to be as many things as they can. What they don't realize is that as soon as they head out to be something else, they open the door for another company to become the specialist. Heinz was a specialist in pickles. Then they became a ketchup. Now they are just about out of a pickle business dominated by Vlasic and Mt. Olive.

Volkswagen was once the specialist in small cars. Then they went big, fast, and recreational. Today the Japanese and Americans dominate this business.

Scott was America's number one tissue, but then became a raft of different paper products. Now Charmin is the leader in tissue.

Beware of the CEO's Hobby

Magna International is a specialist that is a major supplier of parts to the world's top automakers. They have clients the likes of Chrysler, Ford, Jeep, Dodge, Chevrolet, Mercedes, and Cadillac. Their sales are around $6 billion per annum. They are at the forefront of a trend in the automotive industry that has suppliers delivering increasingly larger and more complex parts, such as entire seating systems.

But their chairman, Frank Stronach, is also an avid horse-racing fan who owns hundreds of horses. So it's not totally surprising that the company suddenly picks up some decidedly noncore assets such as California's Santa Anita racetrack. (That's a horse of a different specialty.) Other tracks are under discussion.

Now he wants to move from auto parts to racetracks and sports-gambling operations. Well, it's also not surprising that a lot of shareholders aren't very happy.

Our bet: nothing but trouble.

Tell It Like It Is

Don't make the assumption that everyone knows who the specialist is in a category. One of the things we advise is to position yourself as "the specialist in (whatever)."

People want to know this information because they want to know who is the expert in a business. And if that's all you do, make sure they know it's all you do.

Such was the case with Subaru, a Japanese car company that was having its problems. When George Muller became president in 1993, he asked, "What are we good at?" and "What's our persona?" The answer was, The technology of all-wheel drive.

Right then and there, he decided to focus on that specialty and, as he said, "We made a commitment to sell only all-wheel drive to differentiate ourselves from Toyota and Honda."

And in their advertising they proudly announce that they don't make cars, they specialize in nothing but four-wheel-drive vehicles. It's a move that has turned around a me-too car company that was headed over a sales cliff. (Sales were down by 60 percent from their peak.)

They didn't die, because they used a specialty to differentiate themselves.

Too Many Specialists

Sometimes, just being a specialist isn't enough. Especially if you're surrounded by other specialists.

On the Internet, in a matter of months, you can have an army of specialists in one form of information or another jockeying for their share of "hits" on their Web site.

Consider one of the most popular of the cybercrazes, Web sites devoted to health or maladies. The target market is a big one: cyberchondriacs. Already we have the following sites and their pitches. Okay, class, let's see if you can spot the one with the best chance for success based on the following information:

Medscan Inc. Get your medical information from the site that doctors use.
medscape.com

WebMD Inc. Come for the content, stay for the "community."
webmd.com

Drkoop.com Inc. Trust Dr. Koop.
drkoop.com

American's Health Network. Surgery happens, and you are there!
ahn.com

Mediconsult.com Inc. Information for patients and those who care for them.
mediconsult.com

InteliHealth Inc. Information vetted by Johns Hopkins doctors, presented with flair.
intelihealth.com

AmericasDoctor.com Inc. A doctor is always in.
americasdoctor.com

ThriveOnline. Wellness and the "new health."
thriveonline.com

On Health Network Co. The holistic health site.
onhealth.com

If you guessed that Dr. Koop's Web site has got the best shot, you're right. When it went public, the shares doubled in two days despite the fact that it had all that competition and revenues of just $404,000.

His site has his name and credentials as surgeon general to make it different from all the others. It has a running start because it's different. Most of the others will probably die.

CHAPTER

15

Preference Is a
Differentiating Idea

Our experience is that people don't know what they want. (So why ask them?)

More times than not, people buy what they think they should have. They're sort of like sheep, following the herd.

Do most people really need a four-wheel-drive vehicle? (No.) If they did, why didn't they become popular years ago? (Not fashionable.)

The main reason for this kind of behavior is insecurity, a subject about which many scientists have written extensively.

Following the Herd

Robert Cialdini wrote one of the most interesting pieces of work on why people follow the herd. He talks of "the principle of social proof" as a potent weapon of influence.

135

This principle states that we determine what is correct by finding out what other people think is correct. The principle applies especially to the way we decide what constitutes correct behavior. We view a behavior as correct in a given situation to the degree that we see others performing it.

The tendency to see an action as appropriate when others are doing it works quite well normally. As a rule, we will make fewer mistakes by acting in accord with social evidence than by acting contrary to it. Usually, when a lot of people are doing something, it is the right thing to do.[1]

Social Proof

Supplying "what other people think is correct" is what using "preference" is all about. And what makes preference a very workable strategy is that it comes in many flavors.

Tylenol, the number one pain reliever in America, built its business around the fact that it's the pain reliever hospitals prefer.

Nike, the number one athletic shoe, has built a lot of business around the fact that a lot of famous athletes prefer to use their sneaker. (Because they paid them.)

Lexus, a hot luxury vehicle, built its business around J.D. Powers surveys on customer satisfaction preferences.

Midwest Express Airlines promotes its highest preference rating by *Condé Naste Traveler*.

Science Diet, a premium-priced dog and cat food, is "what vets feed their pets."

People, institutions, media reports, studies—you name it and companies use it. If it smacks of authenticity, it has a chance to separate you from your competition.

"Separating" is a big problem on the Internet, where it's easy to get overwhelmed by all the choices.

Let's say you decide to shop for pet food on the Web. A search engine serves up Pets.com, Petsmart.com, and Petstore.com. When you visit these different "stores," they all seem pretty much the same.

They're all organized by type of pet, have an avalanche of products, and the prices are within pennies of each.

But one site has another weapon to influence you. The first thing you see at the top of Petstore.com's page is an emblem and the endorsement, "exclusive partnership, American Animal Hospital Association." This group is putting its reputation online. (Even if you don't know who they are, it sounds authentic.) That's a herd worth following.

The Rain in Britain

Nobody knows more about umbrellas than the British.

And what's the best of the breed in Britain?

It's arguably the Brigg umbrella, which has been awarded the Royal Warrant as umbrella supplier to the Prince of Wales.

The cachet of swinging the same umbrella as both Prince Charles and *The Avengers'* John Steed will cost you. The Brigg sells for between $200 and $800, depending on your choice of materials.

While most people realize that the royals don't know very much about umbrellas, they do know they can afford the best.

And that's good enough for them.

The Beer in Chile

The Heineken organization built a modern brewery in Chile and introduced a brand of beer called Becker. Their strategy was to bring a high level of quality at more affordable prices, similar to the local market leader, Cristal.

As you would suspect, their market entry was met with fierce resistance from the local brewery. But when the dust settled, research indicated that higher-income consumers preferred the Becker brand. People who appreciate an international quality beer. People who can afford any beer.

Our advice was to use this preference as a way to differentiate with this upmarket segment as well as those who aspire to be part of this group.

This preference was expressed in a simple way: Becker was "preferred by people who can taste the difference."

And who doesn't think they can taste the difference?

No Preference Overlooked

Charles Schwab unleashed what could be called the ultimate preference strategy in an effort to clarify all the claims as to who was the real number one online broker. In a three-page ad in *The Wall Street Journal* they quoted their number one rating by the following independent authorities:

- *Money* magazine rated Schwab.com tops overall with the best online rating—citing "ease of use" and "products and tools" as its two 5-star standouts. *Money* also placed Schwab number one for mainstream investors and wealthy investors.

- *Smart Money* magazine rated Schwab number one for online trading and said, "Schwab simply covered more bases than any competitor."

- *PC World* selected Schwab as a 1999 World-Class Award winner in the Best Web Brokerage Site category, and noted, "Charles Schwab is the undisputed king of online brokers."

- *CIO* named the Charles Schwab Corporation as a winner in its CIO 100 awards, acknowledging the value of building and strengthening relationships with "customers through technology."

- *Financial Net News* selected Schwab overall as 1998 Financial Web Site of the Year.

- *PC Magazine* awarded Schwab excellent ratings in customer support, reporting, and research.

If that wasn't enough, then they wheeled in their number one ratings by independent investors:

- More online investors: Over 2.5 million investors choose Schwab to help them invest online.
- More online trades: Day after day, Schwab handles more online trades than any other broker.
- More online assets.

By the time Schwab was finished, there was no doubt who was the most preferred online broker. In fact, people were afraid to even bring up the subject.

A Questionable Preference

The flip side of the Schwab story can be found in the hamburger wars.

It's an effort that Burger King unfurled to support its famous Whopper when they ran a national television program that claimed the Whopper was "America's favorite burger."

The basis for this claim wasn't sales. McDonald's, with twice as many stores, obviously sells more Big Macs. The basis was a piece of research they sponsored where 700 phone calls were placed around the country and people were asked, "Which one hamburger is your favorite?"

The Whopper was mentioned most often. (They claim 33 percent.)

When your competitor outsells you and your research isn't a well-known independent source and only a third say you're the favorite, we question whether there is enough here on which to build a preference strategy.

Even *The New York Times* questioned this strategy. The opening line in an advertising column discussing the program read: "Is Burger King telling us a Whopper?"

A Legitimate Preference

That "Whopper" raises an important point about preferences.

"What other people think is correct"—the principle of social proof—gets even stronger when your claim stands up to scrutiny. The more legitimate it is, the better.

If you're commissioning your own poll, spend the extra bucks to have a topflight outfit ask the questions.

If you're citing someone else's surveys, make sure their reputation means something. (J.D. Powers and Zagat's are perfect examples.)

If no one has ever surveyed your particular field, try to convince an industry publication to do it. It's a good news story for them, and a potentially great preference story for the winner.

Advertising legend David Ogilvy understood the power of the press in that regard. "Roughly six times as many people read the average article as the average advertisement," he said. "Editors communicate better than ad men."

An Ethical Preference

In some businesses, it's awkward to aggressively promote yourself. Physicians and group medical practices, for instance, would rather not turn their doctors into salesmen.

But patients don't have the sophistication to make complicated medical decisions. (It's hard enough to decide on a Lexus or a Mercedes.) So how are you supposed to wade through the tyranny of choice and pick the right professional?

Once again, "what other people think" can carry the day. It even gets high praise from people who worry about things like doctors advertising.

An ethicist named Randy Cohen described "a better way to meet the admirable goal of helping patients choose a physician." His prescription: "Doctors' medical techniques could be rated by a neutral party, much as the *Barron's* guides rate colleges. Or patient's opinions of bedside could be correlated into a kind of physician Zagat's. Neither puts the doctor in an ethically awkward position."[2]

Preference in Sneakers

Nike has built its reputation and business by spending a great deal of money on athlete and team "partnerships." They have about 4,000 athletes running around in just about every kind of big-time sport in every corner of the world—from Michael Jordan to Tiger Woods to Mia Hamm to Pete Sampras, from 13 major U.S. colleges to 3 national rugby teams to 20 national football and soccer teams. If they're a big name in sports, you probably find a swoosh somewhere on their body.

Their preference strategy can be summed up as "What the world's best athletes wear."

Brooks Sports is also in the athletic shoe market. And while Nike was having some financial setbacks, Brooks has been showing some very nice financial footwork with big sales gains.

Their preference angle is with serious runners. The only people who get their shoes for free are 200 competing runners. While people like Regina Joyce and John Sence aren't household names, they are icons within the running community.

Brooks spends a tiny $750,000 a year on advertising in niche publications such as *Runners World* and *Running Times*. (Nike spends more producing just one of their flashy commercials.)

The moral: If you can't get everyone to prefer you, find a group that will.

The Spirit of Emulation

Long ago, Stanley Resor, one of the founders of J. Walter Thompson Co. advertising, talked about preference in terms of emulation. He said, "We want to copy those whom we deem superior in taste or knowledge or experience."[3]

Once upon a time, European opera stars testified to the beneficial effect Lucky Strike had on their singing. (They sure would sing a different song today.)

Camel cigarettes actually ran an ad that proudly proclaimed that "more doctors smoke Camels than any other cigarette." (Yes, Virginia, that's a real ad.)

The queen of Romania said she entrusted her beauty to Pond's cold cream, and her ad in *Ladies Home Journal* pulled 9,400 coupon replies. (Not to be outdone by a foreigner, an ad featuring Mrs. Reginald Vanderbilt drew 10,300 replies.)

"Nine out of ten screen stars," proclaimed a 1927 ad, "care for their skin with Lux toilet soap."

Later that same year, emulation got overworked. In a single issue of a popular magazine, an actress named Constance Talmadge endorsed eight different products, from inner tubes to alarm clocks.

Today movie stars have been replaced with athletes who can be found endorsing everything from milk to banks to aluminum siding. They are today's heroic figures.

The Importance of "Fit"

Celebrities in Japan and China can make a difference for whatever product is being sold. In the United States there has to be a natural fit or you're wasting a lot of money. People are more sophisticated and aren't that impressed with a well-known name. It has to make sense.

Using the late actor Robert Mitchum as a spokesperson for "tieless" garbage bags was silly. (Inside joke: He never wore a tie.)

Using James Garner and Cybill Shepherd to help sell beef was a disaster. James ended up with heart trouble and Cybill turned out to like veggies more than red meat.

Catherine Deneuve for Chanel. Michael Jordan for Nike. Paul Hogan for the Subaru Outback. They are perfect. Steve Young for milk? We're not so sure.

China Loves Heroes

As we said, whether they fit or not, heroes can mean everything when marketing in China. Local companies now link well-known persons or characters to their advertising displays to differentiate their products from other brands. The Haomen Brewery in Beijing, for example, used a photo of the brewery's president standing with President Clinton for a display in the Wangfujing shopping district.

And, needless to say, powerful figures like the Marlboro man, Mickey Mouse, and Michael Jordan are already in residence.

China Loves Cognac

The Chinese now account for one-fourth of global cognac sales. Its success is based on strong links to modern-day heroes called tycoons. Expensive imported cognac has been positioned as a "social marker," a liquor consumed by China's newly rich.

Aware of the desire of many middle-class Chinese to emulate a tycoonlike lifestyle, Joseph E. Seagram & Sons Inc. introduced Martell Noblige, a midpriced cognac aimed at a new generation of consumers in France, China, Hong Kong, and Taiwan. Just days after the brand was launched, it had become a house brand in more than sixty clubs in China.

People want to drink what the big boys prefer to drink.

An Exercise in Hotel Preference

Just for fun, let's construct a preference strategy for one of the swanky hotel chains. There are two players to consider. The Ritz-Carlton has 22 properties in the United States and 35 total worldwide. A worthy competitor, the Four Seasons, has 21 in the United States and 32 total worldwide.

Condé Naste Traveler magazine, which is geared to affluent travelers, polled 37,000 readers on what they liked the best. (Ladies and gentlemen, unleash your platinum credit cards.)

In a category the magazine called the "best of the best"—the world's 100 finest hotels, resorts, and cruise lines—there were 9 Ritz-Carltons. But there were 14 Four Seasons.

Let's narrow the focus to the best places to stay in the United States: 19 Ritz properties made the list, along with 15 Four Seasons properties.

Business Travel News polled 850 corporate travel planners on fourteen different attributes of deluxe hotels. In first place: Four Seasons. Second place: Ritz-Carlton.

It's a close call, but our statisticians give the nod to Four Seasons. They are the most preferred of the best. They should build a program around being the top choice of people who can afford to stay anywhere they want to stay. They are "the best of the best."

How a Product Is Made Can Be a Differentiating Idea

Companies tend to work very hard in developing new products. Hordes of engineers, designers, and manufacturing people spend endless hours producing and testing what they feel is a unique product that does its job better than anything in the market.

But all that work is often taken for granted by the marketing folks who get swept away in their own activities such as advertising, packaging, and promotion.

We're great believers in digging into a product to find out exactly how it works. More times than not we find a powerful differentiating idea that has been ignored.

The Magic Ingredient

Many products often contain a piece of technology or a design that makes it function. Often, this technology is patented. Yet marketing people tend to dismiss these elements as too complex or too confusing to explain to people. They would rather conduct research and focus on the benefits or the lifestyle experience of the product. Their favorite speech goes like this: "People don't care how it's made. They only care about what it does for them."

The problem with that point of view is that in many categories, a number of products do the same things for people. All toothpastes prevent cavities. All new cars drive very nicely. All detergents clean clothes. It's how they are made that often makes them different.

This is why we like to focus on the product and locate that unique piece of technology. Then, if possible, we give that design element a name and package it as a magic ingredient that makes the product different. And if it's a patented magic ingredient, all the better.

When Crest introduced their fluoride cavity prevention toothpaste, they made sure everyone knew it contained "Fluoristan." Did anyone understand what that was? Nope. Did it matter? Nope. It just sounded impressive.

When Sony started its dominance in television, it made a fuss about "Trinitron." Did anyone understand what it was? Nope. Did it matter? Nope. It just sounded impressive.

General Motors has probably spent over $100 million promoting the Northstar system in the Cadillac. Does anyone understand how this engine works? Nope. Does it matter? Nope. It just sounds impressive.

Magic ingredients don't have to be explained, because they are magic.

High-Tech "Ingredients"

The more complex a product, the more you need a magic ingredient to differentiate it from its competitors.

Silicon Graphics pioneered three-dimensional or visual computing workstations. These were amazing but very complex machines. We discovered that what made all those visuals work was a unique piece of technology called "a geometry engine." We convinced them to take this design element and make it front and center in their marketing programs. It's what made their visual computing workstations not only better but different.

AccuRay is an ABB (Asea Brown Boveri) company that makes quality control systems for the paper industry. Their new system enabled a company to monitor the full sheet of paper as it was being produced. Any imperfections were instantly spotted, which enabled the technicians to quickly make corrections, thus dramatically reducing waste. The benefit of maximum visibility was obvious, but we wanted to know how this all worked. We discovered they had a magic ingredient, which we called a "patented prism technology." Did anyone understand what it was? Nope. Did it matter? Nope. It just sounded very impressive. It's what made their quality control system not only better but different.

Dramatize the Difference

When you've got it, flaunt it.

If you come up with an innovation, make sure you dramatize it. Such was the case of Cordis, which is a Johnson & Johnson company that makes cardiology diagnostic devices.

One of Cordis's most popular (and profitable) product lines for the past six years has been the Brite Tip guiding catheters. Their brilliantly named Brite Tip is a patented, flexible-tip design. It allows cardiologists to easily "visualize" the distal (far) end of the catheter so when they anchor it in the artery that will be getting a stent or a balloon angioplasty procedure, they can "see" exactly where the tip is.

Prior to this, they had to best guess, thus many artery openings were damaged in the process.

The product's differentiating feature—the Brite Tip—was a manufacturing marvel that has now been copied by almost everyone in the industry. Yet Brite Tip still commands 60 percent of market share among at least seven other competitors out there. (That's probably because they've become a generic brand name.)

Product Innovation

Some product ideas aren't buried and aren't magic. If you've got a new wrinkle, you should make it the cornerstone of how you position the product.

Dove bar soap has been the number one soap in North America for years. Its success and its difference are right on the package underneath the brand name: moisturizing lotion. The fact that it's made with moisturizing lotion sets up the benefit of better skin care. But the difference is the lotion in the soap.

A lot of skis promise that you can ski better on that slippery stuff called snow. But one brand has recently developed an innovation that really sets up that benefit of control. The brand is Dynastar and they have what they call a "unique pintail design." They combine product innovation with benefit when they say, "Pintail technology for pinpoint control." Now you have a set of skis with a difference.

DiGiorno Pizza came up with a way to counter the reheating problem of frozen pizza. (It gets cooked twice.) The dough in their pizza has never risen or been cooked. So when you put it in the oven, it actually cooks for the first time. The just-cooked taste puts it on a par with pizzeria pizza. Now you have a frozen pizza with a difference.

System Innovation

There are opportunities to be different by coming up with something that connects to your product or is part of the system.

Black & Decker did just that with its VersaPak innovation. This was a rechargeable battery for use in a number of different tools. They even developed a major program to demonstrate this new and different product by sending VersaPak vans around the country so customers could try out cordless tools with this new technology.

The Granite Rock Company of Watsonville, California, was selling rock and sand to local contractors. (Not a lot of difference in these kinds of products.) Renting trucks to move large quantities of construction materials can cost a dollar or more a minute, so time was important.

To speed things up, the company developed an automated loading system similar to an ATM machine. It accepted an identification card, released the materials, and printed a receipt. They called it the GraniteXpress system and reduced loading time from twenty-four minutes to seven minutes.

Now that is a difference when it comes to buying gravel or sand.

Making It the Right Way

Often, there is a wrong way and a right way to make a product. The wrong or less desirable way is often introduced as a money-saving process. Consultants like to call this "improving manufacturing practices" (translation: cutting costs). The right way absorbs the higher costs so as to produce a better product.

There are times, if an industry is going the wrong way, when you can be different by going the right way. Such is the case of Stanislaus Food Products. They have become the leading manufacturer of tomato sauce for a large number of America's Italian restaurants. And they've accomplished this while charging higher prices. Their strategy was to not follow the industry into concentrate tomato sauce (which is cheaper and easier to ship).

Dino Cortopassi, the owner of the company, felt that fresh-packed sauce, which was never put through the concentrate process, was a better way to make this product. It costs more but it tastes better.

That's his difference. And much to his competitors' dismay, most of the real Italian restaurants in America agree with him.

A Better-Made Pizza

One person who feels that Dino's way of making sauce is the right way is John Schnatter, the CEO and founder of Papa John's Pizza.

He started using Dino's sauce when he was making pizzas in his father's tavern. He continued to use it, despite its higher cost, as he started to build a chain called Papa John's. And because the other big chains use the not-as-good concentrate tomato sauce, John was able to differentiate his pizza by explaining how his pizza was made. The message was very direct: Better ingredients, Better pizza.

Today John has over 2,000 stores. That "how his pizza was made" difference has made Papa John's the most successful pizza chain in America.

Making It Square

There is no better product story than that of White Castle. It's the country's first fast-food hamburger chain and has become an American icon. White Castle sells their square, palm-size burgers (also known as sliders) in more than 330 restaurants in the Eastern and Midwestern United States.

Little has changed in their seventy-odd-year history, from their sliders to their castle-shaped buildings. In fact, the grandson of the cofounder is the CEO.

Their carefully cultivated product strategy has outlasted countless competitors. The result is that they have developed an almost cult-like following that carries on from generation to generation. They even freeze their sliders and ship them to supermarkets in areas where they have no stores.

Their results are amazing. On a per unit basis, they are outsold only by McDonald's. It's a prime example of "steady as she goes."

Making It the Old-Fashioned Way

A similar story comes from Aron Streit Inc., the last independent matzo company. (For those who aren't sure, matzo is the authentic, unleavened, unsalted and un–everything else bread that kept the Israelites alive on their flight from Egypt.)

Even though the company has only a small share of a market dominated by B. Manischewitz, the Streit's Matzo folks realize that "tradition" is just about all that distinguishes one matzo from another. Despite all the trendy outsourcing for many of its other products, Streit's still makes their matzos on Rivington Street in lower Manhattan—the same place the company has made them since 1914.

If you go to Streit's Web site, Streitsmatzos.com, you'll discover that the company knows what the difference is all about. Here's how Streit's puts it: "Why is Streit's Matzo different from other domestic matzo brands? Because Streit's bakes only Streit's Matzo in our own ovens."

They still make their matzo the old-fashioned way.

Giving Up the Old Way

The opposite of the Streit's story is the story of a big ketchup brand in Venezuela called Pampero.

By the time we were called in, Del Monte and Heinz had nudged it from its number one position. Pampero was in a decline. What was needed was a differentiating-quality idea beyond its current claims of "redder" or "better."

Why is it better? What do you do to your tomatoes? After some prodding, what emerged was the fact that Pampero removes the skin so as to enhance the flavor and color. It was something their big competitors did not do in their manufacturing process.

Now that's an interesting idea, as many are aware that most recipes using whole tomatoes call for removing the skin. Pampero could exploit this "without the skins" perception of quality and taste.

When we told them that this was the best and only way to re-build their brand's perception, Pampero became very upset. It seems the company was in the midst of changing to a money-saving automated process that didn't remove the skins (à la Del Monte and Heinz). Pampero didn't want to hear about doing things the old-fashioned way.

Our recommendation was to stop the modernization plans, as "skins off" was the differentiating idea. Doing things like your big-ger competitors is how to get killed in the wars out there.

Charge a Little More

If you have a "better-made" story, you've got the basis to charge a little more for your product. That's what Dino Cortopassi did for his tomato sauce. That also communicates to your customers that your competitors are doing things the cheap way.

That's exactly what Fresh Samantha is doing in the very mature fruit juice category. The secret to their growing share in this mar-ket is to take fresh fruits and vegetables and run them through mas-sive juicers. The result is very expensive, separately packaged fruit drinks. Are they really better than other juice products? Probably not. But America's health-conscious consumer tends to think so. It just goes to show that sometimes the way you make a product can be a way to say you're special.

Handmade in Malaysia

Nothing is as special as making it by hand.

Not too long a drive out of Kuala Lumpur is the factory that makes Royal Selangor. This is a company that makes what many feel is the finest pewter in the world.

A tour of the factory shows you what makes it different. All of it is crafted with great care by hand.

When something is handcrafted (or claims to be), people have a sense that what they're buying is like art. To the customer it makes no difference that the people making these products earn very little. To them they are artisans who take great care and skill in producing these products.

Even if a machine can craft a better product, if it's done by human beings, people feel that it's worth more and it's better.

The ultimate lawn mower is a machine called Locke. Used at the Vatican, Yankee Stadium, and the White House, it bills itself as being built by hand. (They will also send you a bill for $2,500.)

So if you have a chance to talk about anything that's handmade in your product, just do it.

Caskets That Are Different

Batesville is the number one casket maker in America. And no one works harder at being different.

Only Batesville offers "cathodic protection" on their metal caskets. This is the same science that protects the Alaskan pipeline and ships from the ravages of corrosion.

They also offer "Monoseal," which is a system that keeps them from leaking. If you can believe it, each casket is vacuum tested for possible leaks. (That's impressive when you consider how easy it is for them to bury their mistakes.)

They cap all this off by offering a warranty that guarantees some caskets up to seventy-five years.

When Aunt Miriam is buried in a Batesville, her family knows they are burying her in the best and she will be heavily protected from the elements.

Crackers That Are Different

Everyone has grown up with animal crackers. For almost 100 years, Barnum's Animals, the sweet crackers shaped like circus animals, have been a mainstay of Nabisco.

Their unique bright-red-train-car-of-a-box and cracker shapes have been a year-in-and-year-out success despite the fact that little has been done to support this brand over the years.

That's right—no TV, no print, no radio. Yet it's one of the most familiar brands and products in the category.

It's a testimony of how a difference can be all in the making.

Being the Latest Can Be a Differentiating Idea

In this high-tech, rapidly changing world, people have become accustomed to the "next generation" of products. It's not only anticipated, but expected.

Rather than try to be better, we advise companies to try to be next. That's a sure way to be different.

The psychology is obvious. No one is comfortable buying what could be perceived as an obsolete product. So the way to leapfrog your competition is to position yourself as what's new and better (with emphasis on the new).

Making Yourself Obsolete

For years we have preached that strong leaders attack themselves with next-generation products. No one has done this better than Intel.

This march of microprocessors has been a marvel to behold: the 286, the 386, the 486, the Pentium, the Pentium II, the Pentium III, and the Pentium III Xeon. They dominated the sophisticated chip business by constantly introducing the next generation at the expense of their existing microprocessors. That way no competitor has been able to mount an attack, even on price. (Yes, that's a lower price, but it's a lower price on an obsolete chip.)

Gillette's strategy of introducing the next generation of razor blade is also an example of using this approach to dominate a market.

The same goes for GE and its efforts to improve the humble light bulb. Their latest example is a bulb called Enrich. This unique blue glass bulb brings out the vibrant colors in furnishings and decorations by heightening color contrast.

A Ski Boot Saga

Unlike microprocessors, new generations of ski boots don't come along very often. And when they do, it has to be something dramatic to get people out of the old and into the latest. (After all, they've broken them in.)

For those of you who aren't big skiers, Lange is the leading high-performance boot. It's what most professional skiers wear. (A preference differentiator.) But as with automobiles, there are a number of other high-performance boots from which to choose, several of which are perceived as more comfortable.

In what can only be described as a flat market at best, to take business from these boot makers required more than just a new feature. It required a new generation of boot that was more than high performance. (How many skiers race?)

What was needed was a development that made Lange the next generation of boot that would give them a chance to target the entire upmarket segment of ski boots.

A Safety Development

The engineers at Lange started working on a way to solve the 300 percent increase in the number of knee injuries in skiing. In analyzing the problem, they discovered that while skiing was safer than ever, falling backward was the culprit, as the boot firmly held the skier's foot on the ski, thus causing strain and injury to the knee.

To solve the problem they came up with a "rear-release system" that, upon the skier's falling backward, automatically loosened the back of the boot, taking the strain off the knee.

Rather than introduce this as just another feature, we recommended that they introduce this as "a new generation of ski boot that helps protect your knees." What's nice about this concept is that it's broader than high performance. While not everybody races, everyone has a pair of knees.

This new development has only continued their long history of technological developments in ski boots. In 1970, they pioneered the first boot to help protect against ankle injuries. Now, thirty years later, they are pioneering the first boot to help protect against knee injuries. This reinforces their credentials of technological leadership.

A boot that protects your knees sure is a different kind of boot.

The Battle over Acid Stomachs

The drug industry are the masters of next generation. Consider the power of being the latest in the battle for the stomach.

The histamine 2 receptor antagonists (H2RAs) revolutionized the treatment of ulcers and other acid-related diseases when they became available in the mid-1970s. Patients finally had a medication that could heal ulcers, and the need for ulcer surgery plummeted. Tagamet, the first H2RA, generated $1 billion a year in sales at its peak. It was eventually eclipsed by Zantac, which consistently boasted between $2 billion and $3 billion a year in sales. Healthy profits were also enjoyed by the two other H2RAs that the FDA approved in the late 1980s, Pepcid and Axid.

In 1993, the next generation of acid-reducing drugs, the proton pump inhibitors (PPIs), made their U.S. debut with Prilosec. H2RAs and PPIs suppress acid secretion by different mechanisms: The H2RAs block the actions of histamine at the receptors on the gastric cells that line the stomach, while the PPIs decrease the production of acid by deactivating the so-called acid pump inside the gastric cells.

The therapeutic advantages of PPIs over the H2RAs are improved acid suppression and less frequent administration. Early promotional campaigns for Prilosec focused on the drug's mechanism of action.

In 1996, just three years after its introduction in the United States, Prilosec replaced Zantac as the market leader. By 1998, Prilosec had cornered 33 percent of the ulcer drug market and had become the best-selling drug in the world, bringing in $3.98 billion in worldwide sales.

Now looming on the horizon is the discovery of the ulcer-causing bacterium *H. pylori* that could shift therapy from acid suppressors to antibiotics.

In this business, you make hay while the sun shines on your generation.

Break with the Past

The drug industry's new generations have a natural separation, as they are chemically different and usually work differently within the body.

It's important that this "break" be established so as to convince the prospect that this is indeed a new technology. The more the separation, the easier the sale.

This is what's happening in the battle between microwaves and conventional ovens (which the old-fashioned ovens won).

Manufacturers of microwaves are launching a new assault, which will overcome the cooking problems that surround microwave cooking (inedible-looking and unevenly cooked food). They have a new generation of microwaves that use an additional technology that makes food crisp and brown: things like halogen lamps or hot air.

But rather than call them "better microwaves," they are calling them "speed cookers." They hope that this will create the needed break with the past (and they sure do need a break).

Add Another Technology

What you're seeing in the microwave battle is the strategy of adding another technology as a way to create a new-generation product. This is a very effective way to create a difference, as people will quickly see this as an improvement whether they understand it or not. (Two technologies are better than one.)

Milestone Scientific did just this when they added computer technology to, of all things, the very simple hypodermic needle. They created the Wand, which was billed as the first computer-controlled injection system.

The small computer is used to control and deliver the perfect amount of anesthetic, which creates an almost painless injection. (They even had a magic ingredient called SloFlo technology.)

What was most dramatic was the fact that the thumb-controlled hypodermic syringe hadn't really changed much in 150 years. A "new generation" was long overdue.

Dell Computer, the company that built its difference around being "direct," has added another technology. They are bundling in

Web services with their PCs. We call this upping the ante as a way to maintain your difference.

Take Advantage of History

If there has been a history of change in a category and you have been part of it, you should use that to your advantage. If you introduced a prior "new generation," you have enormous credentials to use with your next-generation efforts.

Such was the case with Digital Equipment Corporation, which is now a part of Compaq. They had an opportunity to launch the next generation of 64-bit computer architecture. Unfortunately, they let the opportunity slip away, as did the future of the company.

For those who missed some important computer history, when the entire world was at 16-bit, DEC pioneered the 32-bit VMS operating system and VAX architecture to become the world's second-largest computer company.

So they had a chance to connect the 64-bit workstation to this very successful 32-bit minicomputer. The trick was to take advantage of the fact that the experts said that no one needed 32-bit machines when they arrived. (Wrong.) The same yawns were in evidence when DEC's 64-bit architecture was unveiled. DEC's best strategy would have been to raise the question, Will history repeat itself? If it happened once in history, chances are it would happen again.

And in the computer world, if enough think it will happen, it happens. DEC never made the effort to convince enough people that 64-bit will happen.

The Latest Doesn't Always Work

Now for the bad news. There are some pitfalls in the "next-generation" game that one must avoid at all costs. If you don't, you could have real problems. Here's an outline of what to avoid:

- *Don't solve a nonexistent problem.* Your next-generation product must solve a real problem, not one that's unimportant. Dow Chemical introduced Dowtherm 209, a new antifreeze coolant which was billed as "doing no harm if it leaked into the crankcase" (and by the way, it cost twice as much as old-generation coolants). The trouble was that conventional coolants hardly ever leaked into the engine. Why pay twice as much for a nonexistent problem? Most people didn't.

- *Don't mess with tradition.* There are real problems that people don't want solved. They like the old-fashioned way. Nothing is as traditional as eating unshelled peanuts at the ballpark. Unfortunately, everyone was up to their ankles in shells by the end of the game. To avoid the shell mess, Harry M. Stevens introduced preshelled peanuts in cellophane packages. People were outraged. Sales fell, complaints rose. Back to walking on shells.

- *It must be better.* Why go for the next thing if it isn't a better thing? The United States mint brought out the Susan B. Anthony $1 coin as a replacement for the $1 bill. To the mint it was a big improvement, as they would save $50 million a year in printing and processing costs. To the public there were no perceived benefits. It looked like a quarter and many thought it was ugly. Goodbye, Suzy.

The Latest Can Sneak Up on You

In *The Innovator's Dilemma: When New Technologies Cause Great Firms to Fail*, a gentleman from the Harvard Business School introduces the concept of "disruptive technologies."[1]

The point he makes is that new technologies often arrive as wolves in sheep's clothing. They don't ever line up with your existing customers' needs or Wall Street's expectations of profit. They don't look like much, but once established they improve so quickly that they become a mainstream technology that truly becomes the next thing.

DEC, king of minicomputers, ignored the PC because as a technology it wasn't serious. It was a toy. Well, in not too many years that toy put DEC out of business.

Merrill Lynch was king of the hill with more and more sophisticated services, while Charles Schwab picked off the least attractive end of the market. Schwab has innovated to the extent that they are barely recognizable as a discount broker.

What's Next Should Be Different

The only antidote for disruptive technology appears to be a willingness to set up or buy a completely independent organization to work with this new technology. It could be an independent company or a different brand.

The mistake appears to be trying too hard to cling to the old thing or trying to put the new thing into a company that only knows and understands the old way.

If Kodak feels that electronic cameras pose a threat to traditional film, they shouldn't try to absorb that technology into Kodak. That should be a different company and a different brand. Then let the new organization attack the old one.

Bank One is a large regional bank with 1,900 branches serving a million households in fourteen states. But its ex-CEO, John B. McCoy, saw the disruptive technology of the Internet as a long-term challenge to all his bricks and mortar. So he has launched Wingspan.com, a branchless bank on the Internet, at a cost of $150 million. And he saw Wingspan competing with Bank One. As he observed in *Business Week* magazine, "If you're going to be in E-commerce, you have to build a business that destroys the old brick-and-mortar model."[2]

Being the latest can sometimes be painful, but it's the only way to ensure that you'll have a future.

CHAPTER
18

Hotness Is a
Way to Differentiate

W hen you're hot, the world should know you're hot. As you read in Chapter 15, people are like sheep. That's why they love to know what's hot and what's not. It's also why word of mouth is such a powerful force in marketing. That word of mouth is usually one person telling another person what's hot. This is important, for while America loves underdogs, people bet the winners.

Afraid to Boast

Unfortunately, many companies are shy about telling about their success. First they say that boasting isn't nice. It's pushy. It's bad manners. But what's really behind this reluctance is a fear that they won't stay hot forever. And then what? Won't they be embarrassed?

What we try to explain is that getting a company or product off the ground is like launching a satellite. What you often need is some early thrust to get you into orbit. Once you're in orbit, it's a different game.

Being hot or experiencing sales growth beyond that of your competitors can give you the thrust you need to get your brand up to altitude. Once there, you figure out something else to keep you there.

Corbett Canyon: A Case in Point

To better understand this process, let's go to the world of wine, where differentiation is no easy task.

It's the story of Corbett Canyon, a wine that comes from the coastal canyons in central California. It's a wine that, for openers, selected a uniquely shaped bottle that stands out in the sea of wine you are faced with as you enter a retail store. That was the first difference.

Next, they created a unique radio commercial that used a canyon echo device to make the name more memorable (Canyon, Canyon, Canyon). A unique bottle, a memorable radio commercial, a popular price, and the wine took off. Quickly they became the "fastest-growing wine in America."

The final step was to announce this via their radio program. The natural way to do this is to have a couple discuss what brand is the fastest-growing and to name competitors as guesses. Then you give a "hint, hint, hint." Of course the answer is obvious. It's the wine that comes from those "canyons, canyons, canyons" in central California, a place where wonderful wine can be produced.

Now they have a differentiating idea that could put them in orbit.

Executing a Shift

We must admit that the "canyon" strategy we just developed was a hypothetical exercise. You can't stay hot forever, so you have to get ready to shift your strategy once your momentum slows. In the case of Corbett Canyon, they will have to find a way to explain their success. Whether it's canyons, taste awards, value, or something.

The beauty of a "hotness" strategy is that it sets up a long-term differentiating idea. The marketplace has been primed to believe the story behind your success. Without this last effort, instead of reaching orbit you can fall back and burn-up in the competitive atmosphere.

Hot Chicken

Sometimes trends can make you hot. Such is the case with America's taste buds, which, thanks to the success of Mexican food, are ready for more heat. So spicy chicken is a hot new product category.

Popeyes Chicken serves up Cajun-style fried chicken that is zesty, to say the least. "We're out to save America from bland chicken," say their TV commercials.

Popeyes' $12 million ad budget is puny compared to its giant competitor, the Colonel. But its mouth-watering taste is a red-hot point of difference—enough to drive them past Church's and Chick-Fil-A into the second sales slot in chicken restaurants behind KFC.

All Popeyes should add to their recipe is the fact that they are moving up on KFC, the king of bland chicken. Most people know that Popeyes chicken is hot. Now they should be made aware of the fact that their sales are hot as well.

Lying about "Hot"

You do have to be careful when you start throwing around claims of being "best-selling."

Cadillac got a little egg on its fender when it was forced to admit that it inflated its sales in an effort to maintain its best-selling luxury car status.

They were publicly forced to confess that they had cooked the books in an effort to stay ahead of Lincoln in 1998 sales. This ended their forty-nine-year reign of being the best-selling luxury vehicle.

Not only were they embarrassed, but all the controversy gave Lincoln an enormous shot of momentum and the world discovered who was really hot and who was not.

The point here is that if you're not accurate with your claims, your competitors can exploit your inaccuracy.

Many Ways to Be Hot

When you're using a "hotness" strategy, you have the opportunity to define why you're hot. What many don't realize is that there are many ways to structure that definition. Here's a roundup of the most popular ways:

- *Sales.* The most often used approach is your sales versus your competitors' sales. But don't think it has to be annual sales. It can be any time period you choose: six months, two years, five years. The time you choose to measure is the one that makes you look best. Remember that you are free to pick the parameters. Also, you don't have to compare yourself to your competitors. You can compare yourself to yourself.
- *Industry ratings.* Most industries have annual ratings for performance. They could be industry magazines like *Restaurant News* or consumer magazines such as *U.S. News & World Report* or organizations like J.D. Powers. If you win ratings from one of these, use them as aggressively as possible.
- *Industry experts.* Some industries have experts or critics who are often quoted or write columns. This is especially true in the high-tech world, where you have an Esther Tyson or the Gartner Group. Sometimes you can use their quotes or reports as a way to define your success. Hollywood uses this device to establish a hot movie, as does the publishing world for a hot book.

Every Way to Be Hot

An advertisement for *Fortune* magazine is the epitome of using "hot" as a differentiator. This ad used just about every way to be hot that *Fortune* could put into a full page in *The New York Times.*[1]

They had quotes from industry and business magazines. They had quotes from newspapers. They had a quote from a customer. They had four kinds of sales figures. Then they ended the advertisement with a non–tag line: "*Fortune.* Hotter than ever."

Does the reader know how well *Business Week* or *Forbes* are doing? Nope. Does it matter? Nope. All they know is that *Fortune* seems to be a hot magazine that must be doing something different.

The Press Can Make You Hot

While it's helpful to blow your own horn, it's even better if you can get someone else to do it. This is where an aggressive public relations program can pay big dividends.

What's afoot here is the fact that "third-party" credentials are very powerful. Whether it's your neighbor or your local newspaper, people feel that these sources are unbiased. So when they say you're hot, you must indeed be hot.

Creating a success in public relations is like throwing a rock into a pond. The circles start small but spread throughout the pond. You start with the experts, spread to the trade papers, and expand out to the business and consumer press.

An interview with the CEO of a high-tech Internet service company makes the point about the importance of the press.

How Digital Island Got Hot

Ron Higgins is the CEO of Digital Island, a global Internet service that was created in 1995. It offers corporations a more reliable network with fewer connecting problems and speedier access. It now operates in eighteen countries.

When asked about his success, Higgins attributes it to his public relations. "Public relations," he acknowledges, "is critical. Without it, I know I wouldn't have done nearly as well."

For openers, the first recruit to join the company was a public relations counselor and journalist. Why a PR guy?

His answer: "The role of PR was critical as it was to create an illusion of momentum, to make Digital Island seem bigger than it was, to give it an aura of a Fortune 500 company."

Higgins even put a number on PR success: "Every positive article is worth $1 million in valuation."

His overall feeling: "Without third-party endorsements, I doubt you can be successful in the high-tech industry."[2]

Publicizing a Problem You're Solving

An indirect way to use the press is to entice them to write about the problem that you happen to be solving with your product or company.

If people perceive that you are indeed a part of the solution to a big problem, they will indeed see you growing in importance. And the press does like to write more about problems than successes (bad news versus good news).

Continuing to use the Digital Island story, the problem they were solving was that not everyone around the globe has equal Internet access. In Japan, the Net is very slow and unreliable, as it is in other parts of the world because of traffic overload and the fact that it wasn't designed as an international medium.

That's the big problem that Digital Island was solving. That's a much more interesting story, and it does indeed make Digital Island sound more important.

Growth Can Destroy Differentiation

If there is one culprit in how brands lose their uniqueness, our vote goes to the concept of "growth."

The desire to constantly get bigger seems to be almost a reflex action. We suspect that's because it's at the heart of how people get rewarded. CEOs pursue growth to ensure their tenures and increase their take-home pay. Wall Street brokers pursue growth to ensure their reputations and increase their take-home pay.

But is it necessary? As economist Milton Friedman says, "We don't have a desperate need to grow. We have a desperate desire to grow."

In our view, two bad things happen when companies chase the god of growth. First, they become distracted and miss the opportunity to pour it on and preempt that differentiating idea, or to make it bigger and better.

Problem 1: Distraction

Earlier we wrote about Silicon Graphics and their leadership in high-performance computers. But instead of pouring on the resources and preempting their "high-performance" differentiating idea, they were under Wall Street pressure to broaden their business. To those analysts, high-performance computing is a niche, and not up to a 20 percent per annum growth. This led them into PCs and the less than high performance Microsoft Windows NT operating system. None of these things helped very much.

When you're the Porsche of computers, you don't move into cheaper computers. You dominate the high-performance business by getting more customers to want high-performance computing. (After all, what wealthy company wants low-performance computing?)

Problem 2: Line Extension

The other bad thing that happens is that in an effort to pursue "endless growth," companies fall into what we call the line extension trap. It's typical megabrand thinking, where you hang your brand on as many related or even nonrelated categories as possible. It's what we call "inside" thinking about a successful brand and how to make it bigger and better.

Unfortunately, the only thinking that works in the marketplace is the "outside" thinking that works in the mind of the prospect. Consider what happened to these big companies:

- General Motors had five well-differentiated brands that represented 50 percent of the U.S. business. Each brand, in an effort to grow, started to chase the same business. They ended up priced alike and looking alike. The five undifferentiated brands now represent 30 percent of the business.

- Nabisco had a runaway hit with its SnackWell's devil's food cookies. They quickly added other types, as well as toaster cakes and crackers, none of which tasted as good as their original success. SnackWell's started to run downhill. There has been talk that Nabisco is considering throwing in the towel on the brand.

- McDonald's built a widely successful business on inexpensive, high-speed hamburgers. But then it wanted to become more of a restaurant that offered kids' hamburgers, grown-ups' hamburgers, pizza, chicken—you name it. Now it has become slower and much less successful. It was a "Mc" too far.

Robert Goizueta, the late CEO of Coca-Cola, said, "In real estate it's location, location, location. In business it's differentiate, differentiate, differentiate."

The more things you try to become and the more you lose focus, the more difficult it is to differentiate your product.

Will the Real ESPN Stand Up?

First, there was ESPN—a brilliant idea—a new category in television. But then folks got greedy and decided to extend the line, and ESPN2 was born. Confusing—but it gets worse.

Independent of ESPN, Classic Sports was launched by some enterprising entrepreneurs. The concept behind the new sports channel was to focus on great sporting events in history—kind of a History Channel for sports. ESPN saw it, liked it, and bought it. Did they keep the great name the idea was launched with? Unfortunately, no—ESPN Classic was born instead. Line extension, lost focus, the destruction of differentiation.

Now when people ask to turn on ESPN, the question will be, "Is that ESPN, ESPN2, or ESPN Classic?" The anguished response may very well be, "Oh, forget it. Turn on Fox Sports."

Damaging Your Difference

Marketers fail to realize the long-term damage they do by growing beyond their original identity. They set up serious questions about a brand's difference:

- If Michelob is a first-class premium beer, can it retain its better-taste perceptions with a watered-down light version? Not likely.
- If Volvo is a safe car with tanklike styling, can it suddenly be perceived as a sporty convertible with conventional styling? Not likely.
- If Nike is athletic shoes and clothing, can it suddenly be perceived as an equipment manufacturer? Not likely.
- If Ralph Lauren's tweedy Polo brand is what the preppy groups wear, can it suddenly be perceived as a cool extreme-sportswear brand for mountain bikers, runners, and snowboarders? Not likely.

What happens is that by presenting yourself as something other than what you're known for begins to erode your special difference. You begin to cloud your identity. As you read earlier, minds can lose focus.

Next, you force people to change their mind about what you are about. This is never a good strategy, as people hate to change their mind. As psychologists will tell you, changing an attitude means that a person must change his or her beliefs. (Good luck on that one.)

Finally, you have the problem of becoming that "something else." How is your new effort different? Where are your credentials for that new thing? (Good luck on that one.)

So what you end up doing is undermining your basic identity or difference while, at the same time, you have a hard time selling your new one. Can you succeed that way? Not likely.

Wall Street Rebels

We must be fair about Wall Street. While they do push growth, there are times when they stand up and yell if they think a company has gone over the edge in trying to keep up their growth rate.

They didn't do much when Starbucks started to sell food along with coffee. But it sure happened when they announced plans to focus on the Web instead of finding ways to sell more coffee. As *The Wall Street Journal* reported, "Investors dropped Starbucks Corp. stock like a cup of scalding mocha."[1]

The reason: a growing concern that the infatuation of Starbucks founder Howard Schultz with the Internet may have diverted attention within the company from selling coffee. They just couldn't see Starbucks becoming some kind of cyber-megamerchant where customers go to buy everything from gourmet foods to furniture.

As a senior equity analyst put it, "The discipline is not doing everything but discerning between the nice-to-have business and the need-to-have. Their bread and butter is in their backyard."

We couldn't have said it any better.

Less Can Be More

What companies often do is fail to recognize that maintaining focus on their basic business can work out a lot better in the long run.

If Volvo makes the safest car in the world, why suddenly move into sporty vehicles? Better to look around the world and go where they need safe vehicles. Have you ever driven on a road in India? You sure do want the safest car you can find. The same goes for many roads around the world that are populated with many unsafe drivers and very few policemen.

And what about SUVs? Maybe you can come up with a safer version that does better in crash tests or doesn't tip over so easily.

With the state of the world's roads, we don't see "safety" as a limiting idea. We see it as an idea that still has a long way to go.

(Maybe, now that Ford owns Volvo, they will get back to their own backyard and their differentiating idea.)

Growth via Multiple Brands

But don't think that we're opposed to getting bigger and richer. That's the American way. We're opposed to how people try to do it.

There is a better way.

While you can save marketing money by sticking with one brand, experience has shown that multiple brands can translate to bigger overall market share. Coke and Nike, big single brands, each has about 30 percent of its respective market.

Gillette, on the other hand, has five brands (Trac II, Atra, Sensor, Mach 3, and Good News) and has 65 percent of its market. We call this "the complementary approach," as you have brands that complement rather than compete with one another.

This calls for different names, different positions, and different target audiences. Sometimes you can accomplish the same thing with subbrands. BMW has effectively done this with its 3, 5, and 7 series of cars. They all are "ultimate driving machines," but they are positioned differently to cover different market segments.

A Spanish Multibrand Story

When Spain's national oil company privatized, the new company, Repsol, had three of the country's gasoline brands and about half of its gas stations. There was a new brand created when the company went private (Repsol). Then there was the old, well-known brand of government-owned days (Campsa). Finally, there was a regional brand in the north of Spain (Petronor).

All this would be like one U.S. oil company owning Mobil, Texaco, and Merit: not a bad deal, if you could get away with it.

They had three different names, but all were treated as the same. It was as if they had one brand inside the company and three brands outside.

To protect their 50 percent market share, they decided to differentiate the brands by attribute.

A Brand for the Car

Thanks to a great deal of corporate introductory advertising about the new Repsol brand, most people in Spain gave this new company high marks in the attribute of "innovation and technology." Also, the Repsol brand had pioneered 98-octane gasoline (something even the United States doesn't have). All this tended to set up a strategy that would focus on people who were very car oriented. And since cars are very expensive in Spain, this was a large percentage of people.

The concept that captured this strategy was "Repsol. The best for your car."

Of course, to bring this concept to life they had to focus on car-oriented products and promotion. In addition to 98-octane gasoline, we recommended that they develop a new synthetic oil for today's new engines.

A Brand for Service

Perceptual research showed that the long-term Campsa brand was perceived very favorably. In terms of the attribute of "reliability," it scored exceptionally high as compared to other gas station brands (even 50 percent higher than the new Repsol brand).

This led us to recommend that Campsa take advantage of these perceptions and emphasize its many years of service to the Spanish motorist. The way to express this idea: "Campsa. Sixty years of service."

The way to implement this strategy was to continue to publish their very popular *Campsa Driving Guide* (maps, restaurants, hotels, and so on).

Campsa stations also had begun to put 7-Eleven stores in certain locations. We recommended that they extend these stores to all locations, as well as introduce any new service ideas they had on the drawing board. A typical example of this would be the credit card self-service pumps you see at many stations in the United States.

It turned out that Campsa was also sponsoring a racing program. In this case, we recommended that they discontinue the program and leave the racing to Repsol.

Of course, the Campsa advertising could take viewers through the sixty years of service, thus reminding people of the excellent job they have done for six decades.

A Brand for Price

The last brand was regional, and really had no strong perceptions attached to it. In effect, it had a clean slate in the mind, and could be repositioned in any way the company wanted.

We saw a future possibility for Petronor as a price brand. The way to express this concept: "Petronor. More miles for your money."

In terms of explanation, this brand would be put in high-volume locations, have self-service pumps only, low prices, limited services, and be paid for in cash only.

While price is not yet an issue in Spanish gasoline, this brand certainly could be set up if price wars ever do break out. The point is that sometimes you have to change things today, so that you're ready for tomorrow.

Covering three major segments with three different brands will greatly help Repsol cope with the arrival of the multinational oil companies.

It's how the big oil company in Spain plans to stay the big oil company in Spain.

A Korean Disaster

Daewoo is the second-largest conglomerate, or *chaebol*, in South Korea. And they narrowly escaped becoming the country's largest ever bankruptcy in July of 1999.

South Koreans joke that the motto of their *chaebols* is "from cup noodles to satellites." But saying they have diverse interests is understating the problem. Daewoo is into telecommunications, personal computers, construction, securities, shipyards, hotels, electronics, automobiles, and on and on. There are, count them, twenty-five subsidiaries.

This was growth at its worst as the government leaned heavily on Korean financial institutions to fund the grandiose ambitions of *chaebol* expansion. And while these organizations learned how to make stuff, they never figured out how to sell it at a profit.

With $50 billion in debt, it's no wonder that vultures are circling as various pieces are being sold off. This overgrown conglomerate is in for some serious dieting.

CHAPTER

20

Differentiation Often Requires Sacrifice

A s you read in the prior chapter, wanting too much can be bad for your business. Well, here's the flip side: Giving up some-thing can be good for your business.

Once upon a time there was a company called Emery AirFreight. They were the biggest freight forwarders and their strategy was to offer overnight delivery, two-day delayed delivery, small-package de-livery, and large-package delivery. (Whatever you want delivered, we'll deliver it.) Then along came Federal Express. They sacrificed a lot of business and offered only small packages overnight. Their difference: overnight.

FedEx became a well-differentiated success. Emery went bankrupt.

More Is Less

When you study categories over a long period of time, you can see that adding more can weaken growth, not help it.

In its heyday (about 1980), Miller beer had two brands: High Life and Lite. Their sales ran about 35 million barrels of beer. Then they added Genuine Draft. By 1990, sales had slipped to 32 million barrels. Undaunted, they continued to add more and more Miller brands. Sales continued to go nowhere as Budweiser got stronger and stronger.

Finally, after almost twenty years of "more," their parent company, Philip Morris, came to town and fired the top management of Miller. (What took them so long?)

What Do Cowboys Smoke?

Philip Morris should know a "more is less" problem when they see one. The same thing happened to their flagship brand, Marlboro.

In an effort to maintain growth, Marlboro introduced Marlboro Lights into Marlboro Country. Then they introduced Marlboro Mediums, then Marlboro Menthol, and even Marlboro Ultra-Lights. Suddenly, for the first time in memory, the brand started to turn down.

It's obvious what the problem was about: Real cowboys don't smoke menthols and ultra-lights.

Philip Morris isn't stupid. They are back in Marlboro Country with the red-and-white package. There's not a menthol or medium in sight.

The Basic Problem

The more you add, the more you risk undermining your basic differentiating idea. If, as in Marlboro's case, they stand for full flavor, how can that attribute hold up when you start to offer other flavors or weakened flavors?

Michelob was once a very successful, expensive full-flavored beer. Then it introduced Michelob Light and Michelob Dry. The brand went downhill. Heineken, another expensive full-flavored beer, obviously learned from that mistake. Their light beer was called Amstel Light, which is doing very nicely with the brilliant differentiating idea: "95 calories never tasted so imported."

Once upon a time a company called Eveready had a strategy to offer whatever kind of battery you wanted. Then along came Duracell. They sacrificed a lot of business and offered only alkaline batteries.

Duracell became the specialist in long-lasting alkaline batteries and a differentiated success. But they were not the leader and had nothing to lose. As you saw in an earlier chapter, the need for growth tends to make market leaders vulnerable. Rather than give up anything, they kept adding more. Most failed brands once had a differentiating idea that they destroyed by adding more and more versions. Chevrolet was once a good-value family car. Now what is it? (No one knows.)

What's a Porsche?

When you ask that question, what comes to mind in most people is a mental picture of the famous 911, which is a rear-engine, air-cooled, 6-cylinder car. It's a classic.

But rather than sacrifice, Porsche decided to introduce the 928, which was a midengine, water-cooled, 8-cylinder car that was more expensive.

So now, what's a Porsche? The answer: a front/rear, air/water, 4/6/8-cylinder, cheap/expensive car. Or, to be more accurate, confusion. The result was that sales plummeted to a point that by 1993 the three Porsches were selling about one-tenth of what the 911 sold in 1986.

Luckily, sales are rebounding, thanks to an updated, less expensive version of, you guessed it, the 911.

Convergence: The Latest "More"

Convergence is the opposite of sacrifice, as it is all about products that do more.

And it's hard to avoid predictions about converging products in the worlds of computing, communications, consumer electronics, entertainment, and publishing.

These predictions go way back. A July 18, 1993, cover story in *Newsday* predicted that convergence will cause the eventual demise of videotapes, video stores, newspapers, TV channels, telephone operators, Yellow Pages, mail-order catalogs, college textbooks, library card catalogs, beepers, VCRs, checkbooks, and cassette players.

(We suspect you've noticed that all those things that were predicted to go away are still alive and well. So much for that prediction.)

The latest predictions have telephones, video, and the Internet all converging at our television sets. Even the cartoonists are getting into the act. Our favorite has a gentleman, with his large-screen Sony on his shoulder saying hello into it.

If you study history, convergence rarely happens. Products that do more than they should are quick to die.

Old and New Convergence Disasters

In 1937, we had the convertoplane, a combination of helicopter and airplane that never got off the ground. Neither did the 1945 Hall Flying Car or the 1947 Taylor Aerocar.

In 1961, Amphicar was the first combination boat and automobile. The idea sank. (People figured they could park their boat at the marina and get into their car and drive home.)

In recent times we had AT&T's EO Personal Communicator, a cellular phone, fax, electronic mail, personal organizer, and pen-based computer. Then there was Okidata's Doc-it, a desktop printer, fax, scanner, and copier. Finally we were introduced to a PDA, or

Apple's Newton MessagePad, a fax, beeper, calendar keeper, and pen-based computer.

All of these are no longer with us. In this case, more is dead.

Why Convergence Doesn't Work

Creating products that do more than one thing requires sacrifice of a different kind. Designing multifunctional products forces your designers to give up what could be an outstanding single-function design for a lesser design that accommodates the extra functions.

Can a great car be a great boat at the same time? Of course not. If you want a really fast car, get a Ferrari. A fast boat? Get a Cigarette boat.

Can a great Formula One racing tire be a great passenger car tire at the same time? Of course not. (Racing tires don't have any tread.)

People want the best of the breed, not a mutt that contains several breeds.

People don't want to give up important features so that they can do other things with it. Just because you can build it is no insurance that people will buy it.

If your difference is that your product can do a lot of things not very well as opposed to a product that does one thing exceptionally well, you haven't got much of a difference.

A Future Bank?

First Union National Bank is a regional bank that's into financial convergence. (Maybe you've seen their strange surreal commercials.) Their strategy is to become a financial supermarket offering a "full range of traditional and nontraditional products and delivery channels." (What does all that mean?)

They call this supermarket a "future bank," and they've redesigned its branches to feature telephone kiosks, PCs, and ATMs.

Employees will instruct customers on how to use these new machines in a future-bank mode. In other words, "Come in and use a machine." Unfortunately, their future is off to a bumpy start, as they've had to hire 2,000 tellers in an admission of how they misjudged how much customers want to see real people for their banking needs.

Do people's habits change slowly? Absolutely. Do people want a high-tech financial supermarket? We're not so sure. Will the "future bank" tend to stay out there in the future? Probably. Will all their grand plans work out? Not likely.

Mickey D Wakes Up

McDonald's has recently invested, for the first time, in another restaurant company. Named the Chipotle Mexican grill, it is a tiny but rapidly growing chain that charges $5 apiece for enormous meat-, rice-, and bean-filled burritos. (You won't find Ronald McDonald eating one of these.)

The investment is probably a tacit admission that in today's crowded restaurant field, even the biggest player may not be able to appeal to everyone.

Convergence in fast food just never happened. People go to whom they think does the best job in whatever food they are after. And if we want a pizza, we're sure not going to a hamburger place to get it. And McDonald's McPizza proved that without a doubt.

Different Kinds of Sacrifice

Over the years, we've seen three different kinds of sacrifice that are required in the game of differentiation:

* *Product sacrifice.* Staying focused on one kind of product is far superior to the everything-for-everyone approach (unless you use

multiple brands): Duracell in alkaline batteries, KFC in chicken, Foot Locker in athletic shoes, White Castle in small hamburgers, Subaru in four-wheel-drive cars, Southwest Airlines in short-haul air travel. You can become different as the expert and the best of the breed in this kind of product.

• *Attribute sacrifice.* Staying focused on one kind of product attribute is superior to telling a multiple attribute story. It enables you to be different by taking ownership of a perceived benefit. Volvo took ownership of "safety" in automobiles. Crest took ownership of "cavity prevention." Nordstrom took ownership of "service." Dell took ownership of selling "direct." Your product might offer more than one attribute, but your message should be focused on the one you want to preempt.

• *Target market sacrifice.* Staying focused on one target segment in a category enables you to be different by becoming the preferred product by the segment: Pepsi for the younger generation, Corvette for the generation that wants to be young, Corona beer for the yuppies on their way up, Porsche for the yuppies who have made it.

When you chase after another target segment, chances are you'll chase away your original customer.

Whatever you do, you should not get greedy but stay true to your product type, your attribute, or your segment.

How to Feel Good about Sacrifice

When companies are told they have to sacrifice, they often get very upset with the idea. After all, no one really wants to give up anything or get locked into what they feel is a limited market.

But then we let them in on the good news. It goes like this: What you advertise, what you sell, and what you make money on can be three different things.

Let's take Burger King as an example. They should advertise "Broiling, not frying," because that makes them different from

McDonald's. Once people arrive, they can sell them chicken or fries or whatever. Who cares? And as for making money, that comes from selling soft drinks, which certainly doesn't need advertising.

You get the idea? In many cases, the sacrifice is found primarily in how you communicate or craft your message to the marketplace as to why you're different. Once you capture those prospects, you're free to sell them whatever. And how you make your money is yet another issue.

So, while "sacrifice" limits you in how you present yourself to attract customers, you're not really limited in what you sell them once they are in the door. (Federal Express does handle packages that don't just go overnight.)

Now, don't you feel a little better?

Being Different in
Different Places

Go global, young man. That was the advice from Theodore
Levitt when his seminal article, "The Globalization of Markets," was published in 1983. Since then, globalization has
become a dominant theme of international business strategy.

It really is a neat idea: You drive a global brand with one big differentiated idea, everywhere from Akron to Auckland. Your brand
gets recognized on the shelf by travelers and natives alike. A single
marketing team means you save on staff and time. A single global
name and design lowers production and manufacturing costs. The
same pool of commercials used everywhere means you save on production dollars. (And your ad agency is happy, too: They have less
work to do.)

Seldom has one concept been so overused and misused.

Play It Where It Lies

Like marketing, golf is a global game, too. But early on, golfers learn something that many marketers ignore: You have to play it where it lies.

The idea of marketing a standardized product with a uniform message around the world remains "purely theoretical," according to the president of the Hellenic Institute of Marketing in Greece. Although a product concept may be universal, it must be adapted to differences in local culture, legislation, and even production capabilities. Consumers' interests and needs are not the same everywhere.

And let's not overlook local competition. By the time you show up on the other side of the globe, a local firm may have preempted your differentiating idea.

The Finnish Coffee Caper

That was the case in Finland, a little country with a big coffee habit. Finns are among the world's heaviest coffee drinkers, with an average consumption of 160 liters per person.

General Foods targeted Finland with its Swedish coffee brand, Gevalia, a blend of Colombian, East African, and Indonesian beans. (Gevalia's label proclaims that it serves "His Majesty the King of Sweden and the Royal Court.") But the megamarketer's entry was thwarted by the decades-old local brand, Paulig coffee.

In Finland, Paulig owns the high ground in coffee. It's the original. It tastes good. It owns the social occasion. (The social aspect of coffee in Finland is important, as well as treating yourself to a cup of coffee after a job well done.)

So was there room for a standardized coffee product with a universal message? Not in Helsinki. Paulig, the home-grown brew, kept perking along with its more than 50 percent share. Gevalia barely made a dent.

The Universals

Yes, there are some universal aspects to life and marketing.

Oil of Olay was the first beauty product to say a woman can be beautiful at any age, and that idea speaks to women the world over.

Some companies can turn their national origins and heritage into global identities (as long as they've got the massive budgets to fan the flames). Levi Strauss and Disney export the American dream. Chanel and Louis Vuitton represent French chic. Armani represents Italian style. Burberry stands for classic English values.

But for most marketing mortals who are chasing "one global village," the facts just don't support the dream.

A Global Pioneer Finds There Are Limits

Nestlé has been a global company from its earliest days. In the 1860s, pharmacist Henri Nestlé worried about the dying children. (Infant mortality was higher in Switzerland than in most emerging countries today.) He developed one of the first Nestlé products, an infant cereal to help feed them.

Henri Nestlé had two grand visions. First, he immediately went international. The product was in five European countries four months after launch. Second, he wanted his own brand. Store brands (private labels) already existed, but he was one of the first to create a manufacturer's brand.

But even with its potent global thrust, Nestlé has realized over the years that global brands alone can't win the war.

An analysis a few years ago by the McKinsey consulting firm showed that the company regularly sends out different horses for different courses. Nestlé has:

- Several dozen worldwide brands, such as Baci, Buitoni, Carnation, Kit Kat, Maggi, Mighty Dog, and Perrier (the U.S.P.s vary by country).

- More than a hundred regional brands, such as Alpo, Contadina, Herta, Mackintosh, and Vittel (no globality here).
- More than 700 local brands, such as Brigadeiro, Solis, and Texicana (not even close to global).

Hold the Beef, Please

McDonald's cholesterol kitsch comes from its American origins and heritage. The icon of the golden arches wants to think globally, but it is forced to act locally.

Consider the following:

- In Germany, the second-largest market outside the United States, there are different challenges. Menus are much more varied (Oriental Burgers) and there are more vegetarian offerings (Veggie McNuggets).
- In Italy, there's a special espresso counter at McDonald's where you can buy hot drinks.
- In China, commercials use children to explain to the older generation what McDonald's is all about. (There is no heritage to import.)
- But in Australia, which has one of the highest concentrations of outlets per mouth in the world, McDonald's reinforces its U.S. credentials with commercials featuring dead American stars such as Marilyn Monroe and James Dean.

Says the international account director for Leo Burnett, which has handled the McDonald's brand in eighteen countries: "Marketing food is a tricky business precisely because everyone has an idea of what good food should be, and it's usually a different idea. The U.S. overtones of a McDonald's sandwich might be aspirational in Latin America or even some of the Asian markets but, by the same token, these overtones are guaranteed to make European hackles rise and trigger complaints about American culinary cultural imperialism."[1]

Which probably explains why McDonald's commercials in the UK tend to focus on the qualities of the food rather than their American heritage.

Beer That Travels

Heineken is a global beer.

The world's second-largest brewer is meticulous about product consistency. All its breweries stick to the same recipe. To make sure the product is the same everywhere, every fourteen days their breweries send samples to professional tasters in the Netherlands. The company also buys back bottles from small shops as far away as Shanghai for testing.

Employees are not permitted to alter a single line on the label, lighten the packaging colors, or vary the shape of the bottle. (Step out of line by one iota and you go directly to Heineken hell.)

But what about the differentiating idea for this premium beer? Standardizing the taste is one thing. Karel Vuursteen, Heineken's CEO, admits that standardizing the marketing is impossible.

Says Vuursteen: "We don't believe you can communicate to all cultures in the same way. In the United States and Western Europe beer is a normal part of life, it's thirst-quenching. In Australia and New Zealand, it's very macho. In many Southeast Asian countries, it's almost a 'feminine' product—sophisticated. Thus, we give our local representatives a lot of freedom in sales and advertising."[2]

Different in India

This is the land of nonstandard marketing.

You say you want to take your products to India and get a piece of that big middle class (260 million Indians).

Be careful, there's still not a lot of money around. The median household income is still only $833 a year. At that level, a cheap television and a cheap sewing machine are the best families can do.

Sure, people buy cell phones, but to keep costs down they note the number calling and ring back on a conventional phone. Average usage is less than five minutes a month.

To deal with this world, you have to make your products afford-able. You sell very small cigarettes or packets of toothpaste that cost just a few cents.

Reebok sells $23 running shoes. Kentucky Fried Chicken has gone to India with budget-priced meals and local vegetarian and spicy dishes. (Sales are up 200 percent as a result.) McDonald's sells the Maharajah Mac (two all-mutton patties). GE-Godrej, an Indo-U.S. joint venture, recognized that home appliances double as status symbols and have been successful by producing attractive re-frigerators that look good in the living room.

To sell in India, you have to do it India's way, not your way.

Some Rules for the Road

Before you decide that one differentiating idea can take your brand around the world, here are some things to keep in mind:

1. *The current idea may be the wrong idea.* Sometimes, you'll do better by bringing back an old idea.

   For reasons we'll never comprehend, Coke moved away from "the real thing," its powerful message that there's only one original and all the other colas are just copycats.

   But in Russia, there's a rediscovery of roots and a respect of authentic things. So in Moscow, "Drink the legend" is Coke's national TV and poster campaign. It's the real thing, in a new translation.

2. *Attributes can change when you cross borders.* As you read ear-lier, the attributes of beer itself can range from macho to fem-inine, depending on local customs.

   The attributes of an individual brand can change, too. In Mexico, the Corona brand is a humble, low-rent beer. You can pick up a six-pack in a Mexico City *supermercado* for about $2.50. But in the United States, Corona has a spring-break, palm-trees, drink-it-with-a-lime upscale image. That same six-pack will cost you $6 in Atlanta. Much to the bewilderment of Mexicans, Corona is now the top-selling imported beer in the United States.

Or consider yogurt. In the United States, yogurt is generally seen as a healthy food, and the Dannon brand celebrates that. But in France, Danone was seen as too indulgent, too pleasure oriented. So the company created the Institute of Health, a real research center dedicated to food and education.

3. *Your market leadership may not translate.* Nescafé is Nestlé's top-selling coffee brand around the world.

   But in India, Nestlé had to create a special instant coffee named Sunrise to please local taste buds.

   Sunrise is blended with chicory to give a strong and familiar flavor. Sunrise outsells the world-famous Nescafé in India.

4. *Your heritage may not be respected.* Kellogg's is a proud old name for cereal. But the folks from Battle Creek got a cold shoulder in India, where hot food is preferred for breakfast because Indians believe it infuses them with energy. (Indians believe food shapes personality and mood.)

   So much for heritage.

5. *Your specialty may get blurred.* What's Lux? Well, you see the name throughout Asia, usually accompanied by sexy American stars with box office appeal. (Celebrities such as Demi Moore, Liz Taylor, and Brooke Shields hawk Lux products.)

   In Indonesia, Lux is a soap.

   In China, Taiwan, and the Philippines, Lux is a shampoo.

   In Japan, it's everything from soaps to shampoos.

   It's tough to convince the world you're a specialist when your expertise varies according to geography.

One for All?

The client services director for a global design firm says: "The same branding is reassuring, but it can mean different things in different markets. The benefits seem to be mainly for the companies. They save on economies of scale. They have fewer people thinking strategically about the brand."[3]

And that's the problem with all-out globalization. Tastes vary. Preferences vary. People vary.

You can differentiate anywhere.

But you can't differentiate everywhere with the same idea.

Maintaining
Your Difference

As you just read in earlier chapters, the desire for endless growth often leads to the "everything for everybody" trap. This, in turn, leads to the end of differentiation. (We won't bore you with any more examples.)

But there are some important guidelines to maintaining your difference—guidelines that can help keep you from wandering off into the wilderness and getting lost.

Remember Your Difference

When companies or brands are being built, management is usually very involved with the essence or difference of a product or service. But as time goes on and new management arrives, that difference can be in jeopardy as new egos come into play and corporate memory begins to fade.

Somehow you must find a way to maintain the understanding of your difference with ensuing generations of management. You can't let them wander off strategy. That's exactly what General Motors did with their brands when, for financial reasons, they began to price them alike and make them look alike.

That faulty memory led to a dramatic loss of market share.

The Sears Story

Sears is a legendary retailer under attack. Wal-Mart, Kmart, Target, Home Depot, Ames, Circuit City, and a host of other retailers are making their life and future very difficult.

Being different is critical in an overretailed world. But how do they do it? If you study what made Sears successful, you realize that they were the first and only retailer to build major brands: Kenmore appliances, Craftsman tools, DieHard batteries, Roadhandler tires, and Weatherbeater paint. These were very good products at very good prices and they were guaranteed. And they were only available at Sears.

History tells you that it's these brands that makes Sears different. So their future depends on maintaining the strength of these brands and doing what they did in the past: Build some new ones.

Remembering what made them successful is the key to differentiating Sears.

Stay Contrary

Bob Lutz, the president of Chrysler, wrote a book called *Guts*. In it is a chapter that's worth the price of the book. It's titled "When Everybody Else Is Doing It, Don't." We couldn't have said it any better. Being different often requires "going against" thinking. You have to have the guts to go against what is often conventional wisdom.

As we wrote in an earlier chapter, when a nineteen-year-old named Michael Dell started his own little computer company, he knew he couldn't compete with established companies for floor space in stores. However, the rules of the industry, at that time, dictated that computers had to be sold in stores. Every company in the industry believed that customers wouldn't trust a mail-order company to provide such a high-end item.

Michael Dell broke the rule. He ignored conventional wisdom in the industry and direct-marketed. And in no time he built a billion-dollar company.

Most organizations believe the way to succeed is to emulate the most successful members in their given category. So they begin to drift away from their difference in search of the business that a competitor already has in hand. Pepsi dropped its "new generation" focus for an everybody focus. Burger King goes after the little kids that belong to McDonald's. Cadillac keeps trying to sell small Cadillacs to the younger set.

What these companies fail to realize is this: "Once contrary, always contrary."

A Contrary Move in Jet Engines

One of the best ways to be contrary is to redefine the business and the way it's done.

Beset by earlier technical problems, the GE90 jet engine has run a distant third behind Pratt & Whitney and Rolls-Royce to power the Boeing 777. So when the new 777X long-range version of the plane was being developed, General Electric saw an opportunity to redefine the business. The strategy came in two parts.

Part one was to convince Boeing to sell the plane as a package—aircraft and engines. This is a break from the normal practice where Boeing sells the aircraft to the airlines, which then makes an engine decision (GE, Pratt & Whitney, or Rolls-Royce). GE pulled this off with a unique preset cost of so many dollars per flight-hour maintenance deal that takes the risk out of maintenance costs for the airline.

Part two was an agreement by General Electric to pick up half the development costs for the new version, thus taking from Boeing some risk of meeting performance guarantees.

In return for this new approach, Boeing made GE the exclusive engine supplier for this long-range aircraft. At about $12 million a copy, that contrary move by GE could be worth $20 billion in revenue over the coming twenty years.

Be Consistent

Once you've established what makes you different, your next assignment is to reflect that difference in everything you do. This single-mindedness will influence not only your customers but your own employees as well.

Consistency comes in many forms. One form is consistency of message. Often companies develop a simple but effective differentiating message, which shows up in its advertising. But the public relations people head off in a different direction. Then you have the promotional people who want to do their thing, which is the same for the corporate affairs people who are talking to stockholders and Wall Street.

Instead of each group running with the same idea, they want their own ideas so that they can get the credit for their work, not someone else's work.

The only person who can keep everyone pointed in the same direction is the CEO. He or she has to keep everyone focused on the same message.

Making the Tough Calls

If, as we wrote earlier, Burger King were to focus on older kids, the CEO would have to go to the franchisees and make sure they get rid of their swing sets. The CEO would say to the product people, "No more kiddie meals," and to the promotional people, "No more Disney tie-ins." The CEO would go to the advertising people and the agencies and say, "We're a grown-up place and McDonald's is a kiddie place. All of our messages for the foreseeable future should drive this idea."

Finally, he would have to have the guts to go to Wall Street, the board, and the stockholders and explain why the company is walking away from the kids-and-family segment. (This is all very tough stuff, which is probably why the company never pursued this strategy which we presented to them years ago.)

Consistency in Operation

Earlier we mentioned Wells Fargo bank and their use of heritage to differentiate themselves around the attribute of speed of service. The concept: "Fast then. Fast now."

But to take ownership of that difference, the bank will have to do a lot more than just run an integrated communications program. They will have to work very hard at developing fast responsive services.

They also will have to build a very aggressive internal program to make their people more sensitive to being responsive to customer needs. The promise of being "fast" requires that you deliver on this promise. And your customers will quickly notice any inconsistency.

Years ago, when Avis proclaimed that they "try harder," their people had to exhibit that kind of effort.

Or when United set out to have "friendly skies," their personnel had to keep that smile on their faces, no matter how angry the passengers. (We suspect that this program was dropped because being friendly after a several-hour delay is impossible.)

Again, maintaining this kind of consistency is in the hands of the CEO. He or she has to be the cheerleader in this consistency effort.

The most friendly and funny skies in the airline business belong to Southwest Airlines. What makes that happen is CEO Herb Kelleher. When you see Herb on a plane, he is the funniest of the lot.

Stay Connected

There are times when you have to change your position. The market has shifted underneath you, and either you're onto another differentiating idea or you're dead. That is what kept Lotus alive when Microsoft took over the spreadsheet business with Excel for Windows.

But this is usually an exception, not the rule. More times than not, your program should be a continuous effort to maintain and even improve your difference. Change because the marketplace changes is one thing. Change for the sake of change is another. Some of this happens when you pursue endless growth.

Implementing endless product variations, just to pump sales, only clutters the shelves and shifts the balance of power to the retailer who owns the shelf space. (Consider the cough/cold remedy aisle in your average supermarket. There are so many variations you can't even find what you're looking for.)

Running out endless line extensions just to get bigger numbers only mucks up brand perceptions and opens the door for specialized and well-differentiated competition. The beer business has regular, light, draft, dry, and now ice beers. It's no wonder the only growth in recent years has been in the microbrewery segment.

Evolve Your Difference

Crest toothpaste has been one of Procter & Gamble's main brands for many years. They have owned the attribute of "less cavities" for over thirty years.

But thanks to fluoride in water, where the average person once had 15 cavities in the early 1960s, that number had dropped to 3 cavities in the early 1990s. As a result, the cavity prevention attribute was losing its power. Tartar control and gingivitis protection were becoming more important attributes.

What Crest should have done is what we call "evolving your difference." In other words, broaden their difference but do it in a way that stays connected to their past. The obvious move was for Crest to reposition themselves as the "pioneer in tooth care" and to introduce a new Crest that dealt with cavities, tartar control, and gingivitis.

Unfortunately, that's exactly what Colgate did with their new Total product.

We're afraid that when it comes to Crest, there is no joy in Cincinnati these days. After more than thirty years, Colgate is back in first place.

Don't Just Sit There

What this illustrates is that the market is a changing place and your difference often needs some adjusting.

Toys "R" Us created a unique format—a warehouse packed with every kind of Barbie and Hot Wheels imaginable. It drove its nearest competitors into bankruptcy and had things pretty much locked up.

What happened next was described in *Fortune* magazine:

> But then the world changed. Now Toys "R" Us has much tougher competitors: Wal-Mart and the Internet. Wal-Mart sells Pokémon, Furby, Barbie and Hot Wheels—most of the toys that Toys "R" Us has—at cheaper prices. A harried mom wandering the aisles at Toys "R" Us told me, "I don't usually come here. I'll just pick something up when I'm at Wal-Mart." And whatever you can't find at Wal-Mart, chances are you can now find it on eToys or Amazon.com.[1]

Unfortunately, Toys "R" Us still dwells in their glory days and still clings to their old format. They haven't evolved their difference.

Now that Wal-Mart sells more toys, Toys "R" Us might consider *Fortune* magazine's suggested name change: Toys "Were" Us.

An Irish Legend

Waterford crystal is one of the best-known and highly perceived brands in the category.

But pricing trends have threatened to push the brand into a Rolls-Royce category: very nice but very expensive. And at $40 to $50 a glass, the potential for breakage becomes a strong inhibitor. There is no shortage of less expensive crystal from which to choose (and to drop).

Should they just sit there, or is there a way to get around this pricing problem? Our vote was "evolve the brand." The strategy was to introduce a "lifetime replacement program" for Waterford tableware that is accidentally broken. The offer was a low replacement cost of one-half the list price.

The program was simple. A registry number is assigned to a purchase of tableware. When a glass is broken, this number as well as the "Waterford" mark are returned to the factory. A replacement goes directly to the customer. The program is doable because it eliminates the retailer. This way, a "one-half list price" would probably generate a small profit or break even.

This "evolving" concept could be expressed by positioning Waterford as "an investment for life."

Did they do it? No. What they did instead was introduce a cheaper "By Waterford" line extension brand.

The moral here and in the Toys "R" Us story is that evolution requires change that is not always very comfortable for people to embrace.

Evolving versus Tinkering

There's a big difference between evolving a brand and fooling around with it. Evolving usually addresses a competitive move or a serious change in the market.

Tinkering usually involves cosmetic changes or silly line extensions or efforts to exploit a trend. It's also how offices full of marketing people keep from getting bored. Consider the following.

Someone on the Prell shampoo brand says, "Hey, why don't we add a blue Prell to our line of green Prell?" Of course this ignores the consumer perception that if it isn't green, it can't be Prell. It's what makes Prell different.

Bad idea.

Someone on the Pepsi brand says, "Hey, why don't we take advantage of the New Age purity fad, and introduce a clear Pepsi? We'll call it Crystal Pepsi." Of course this ignores the consumer perception that if it isn't brown, it's not going to taste like a cola. And isn't Pepsi the best-tasting cola?

Bad idea.

At McDonald's someone says, "Hey, let's take advantage of the pizza trend and add McPizza to the menu!" Of course this ignores the consumer perception that hamburger joints can't know much about making pizza. And aren't they the folks that have made billions of hamburgers?

Bad idea.

Someone at Anheuser-Busch says, "Hey, why don't we add dry and ice beers to our lineup?" Of course this ignores the consumer perception that beer is usually wet and not served over ice. And doesn't this all clash with their wonderful heritage? Would grandfather have done this?

Bad idea.

Differentiating has got to line up with the perceptions in the mind, not go against them. What people inside the company perceive as "improvements" only cause confusion inside the mind of the prospect.

They undermine your difference.

Who Is in Charge of Differentiation?

Top management has to be in charge of making sure that a differentiating strategy is generated, communicated, and maintained. In other words, the CEO has to be involved.

And yet, all too often the "right strategy" is taken for granted. Top management assumes that all those experienced marketing people and advertising agencies have all that stuff worked out. So they go back to working on their problems with the board or making sure that next year's numbers look good.

And the problems begin.

Why CEOs Fail

Fortune magazine let some management guru write about what the magazine called failed CEOs. Their definition was executives "that were pushed, saw their company bought or left a company that had lost its way."[1]

In this analysis, the author didn't even list "bad strategy" as one of the "six habits of highly ineffective CEOs." And, in fact, he went on to say that the majority of problems were caused by bad execution, not high concept boners. To *Fortune*, if you put the right person in the right job, all will be well.

We're not so sure about that. When we looked at their lineup of CEO failures, we saw more lousy strategy than lousy execution. Here's a sampling:

Robert Allen (AT&T, 1988–1997). Here's a CEO who never took advantage of AT&T's leadership position, which was the ultimate differentiator. Instead he tried on several occasions to get the company into computers. The efforts failed and cost billions. Bad strategy.

Joseph Antonini (Kmart, 1987–1995). He tried to compete with Wal-Mart on price and lost. It's tough to go against an organization like that without a structural advantage. He needed a strategy beyond price to attract people to Kmart. He had none.

Al Dunlap (Sunbeam, 1996–1998). From his performance, Chairman Al wouldn't know a good differentiating idea if he fell over it. All he knew how to do was pass out his book, cut costs, and try to dazzle Wall Street. All show and no strategy.

Carl Hahn (Volkswagen, 1982–1992). Hahn watched VW's market share in the United States plummet while he tried to sell fast, big, expensive VWs to a market that wanted small, economical, and reliable VWs à la Beetle. Those were the attributes that they owned in the mind. He stubbornly pursued a failed strategy.

Arnold Langbo (Kellogg's, 1992–1999). Too many brands, too many businesses such as bagels and frozen lasagna, inflated prices, and no reason as to what makes Kellogg's the best cereals. Very little strategy.

Robert Palmer (DEC, 1992–1998). Palmer failed to execute a "being the latest with 64-bit" differentiating strategy. It was DEC's only hope to stay alive. This lack of a next-generation strategy is why DEC, as a company, is no longer with us.

Michael Quinlan (McDonald's, 1987–1998). Quinlan fell into the "everything for everybody" trap and failed to use their hamburger leadership to full advantage. McPizza, McLean, Mac at Night—it was all a "Mc" too far and very little strategy.

John Sculley (Apple Computer, 1983–1993). Sculley failed to pre-empt and maximize the ease-of-use attribute that Apple enjoyed in both their operating system and their PCs. He was slow on the next generation, and he bet big on the overcomplicated Newton and lost. He should have stayed at Pepsi.

Robert Stempel (GM, 1990–1992). Stampel inherited a company that had destroyed its well-differentiated brands by pricing them alike and making them look alike. He didn't recognize that this was a losing strategy. In no time he was toast.

Missing the Point

So what does it take to get things done? Says the article in *Fortune:* "People first, strategy second." In fact, "Strategy is less than half the battle."

Talk about missing the point by a country mile.

Whatever happened to having the idea first, then assembling the people and machinery to make it a reality?

The strategic idea—the differentiating idea—is easily half the battle, not to mention the more important half.

Without the powerful single idea, all the motivation and people skills in the world aren't going to help.

The problem with articles like this is that *Fortune* lets some guru with a consulting business make a case for what just isn't true. And what's worse, it encourages others to take good strategy for granted.

What Really Went Wrong?

You can quickly see what happened. This group of executives didn't have execution problems, they had "what to do and not to do" problems. And they were probably misled by a lot of high-priced managers armed with brilliant presentations and big promises.

The problem with many companies is that top people often don't get involved in the strategic process. When we presented the "64-bit strategy" at DEC, Bob Palmer was nowhere to be found. He didn't go to meetings like that. Well, maybe he should have, because a CEO has to understand what's on the table and what his options are, if any.

Most big moves often challenge old businesses. The result is a reluctance to foster the new ideas. Peter Drucker calls this "slaughtering tomorrow's opportunity on the altar of yesterday."

Why CEOs Must Be Involved

What you encounter often in the midlevel of companies are people with a bad case of "personal agenda." They are trying very hard to put their mark on something so as to progress up the corporate ladder. They make their decisions based not on what's good for the company but on what's good for their careers.

Or worse than that, they are trying to avoid mistakes that could put their careers in peril.

We once developed a strategy for a company that essentially challenged their soon-to-be-announced effort to try to sell a new generation of computer systems. At the end of the session, an executive looked me in the eye and said: "Where were you when I needed you two years ago?" (Two years ago this bad decision was sent to the board of directors for initial approval.)

Even though this executive now realized it was the wrong decision, he was saying that he couldn't admit to a mistake of that magnitude. Understandable from his point of view, but tragic from the company's point of view. Especially when you consider that a competitor took the same strategy and built a multibillion-dollar business around it.

Only the CEO was in a position to change the plans, and he wasn't in the room.

"I'm in Charge"

Another problem you may encounter is the "corporate ego" of your managers or your advertising agency. There might be an interesting "outside" idea on the table, but they may have a problem with an outsider doing their job. "After all," they'll say to themselves, "I'm in charge. If I accept someone else's thinking, my superiors will think less of me."

This can be a very difficult situation. We've discovered that, rather than dismiss an "outside" recommendation out of hand, this type of person invariably adds his or her own thinking to the situation. Makes his or her contribution, so to speak. What results is a modified strategy that isn't really the same. It's like changing a cake's recipe—it may look the same, but it sure doesn't taste like the same cake. (Advertising agencies are especially good at this kind of modification.)

The higher you are presenting in an organization, the less likely you are to come across these kinds of ego problems.

One That Went Right

Jim Manzi, the former CEO of Lotus Development Corporation, was also faced with a bleak future. Microsoft had preempted the next generation of spreadsheet software. Their 1-2-3 spreadsheet was in trouble, as was Lotus.

Microsoft Excel had a big difference with its Windows operating system.

Manzi went to the meetings, listened to the outside ideas, and decided to pursue the recommended "groupware strategy," or software for networks of computers. His difference was that he was first with a software called Notes, the first successful groupware program.

Five brutal years later and at a cost of half a billion dollars, Jim Manzi had the next big thing and the momentum to go with it.

IBM bought the company for $3.5 billion and everyone was happy. The right strategy paid off.

The Best Do Their Own

When you study success, you tend to find that the best CEOs do their own strategy. Herb Kelleher at Southwest Airlines, arguably the industry's most successful airline, calls the shots. And no one is better at being different than Herb.

Jack Welch certainly can't run a company the size of GE by going to the meetings and being involved with strategy. But he has extraordinary longevity in top executives. Almost all of his team have been running the different business units for an average of twelve years. He trusts his top people to figure out how to be different.

John Schnatter of Papa John's Pizza does his own strategy, as we suspect does Bill Gates of Microsoft. And we're sure that Martha Stewart calls the shots on her rapidly spreading decorating and lifestyle empire. These are young entrepreneurs who are building their businesses and they don't trust their strategy to middle-level executives. (Can you blame them?)

A Success from Finland

In 1992, forty-one-year-old Jorma Ollila was made CEO of a struggling Finnish conglomerate named Nokia. He unloaded pieces of the old company, such as computers, cables, and TVs, and concentrated its resources on mobile communications. He sensed that with some sacrifice, Nokia could seize a leadership role.

He set out to be different. As the digital phone standard took off in Europe, he was ready with easy-to-use phones equipped with the very different trademark TV-shaped screen. New differences were quickly introduced, such as longer-life phones, fashion colors, and even customized differences for major markets (louder rings in Asia, different standards, voice recognition where keyboards are a problem).

Quickly Nokia built up the perception of being the most advanced mobile phone on the market. (Nice difference.) Now Nokia is the world's leading mobile phone. (A better difference.)

Ollila is in charge of keeping Nokia different. To do it, he pushes the company to churn out new models of phones at a dizzying rate. He's laying infrastructure for a new wider-bandwidth wireless technology called "the Third Generation." (Analog and digital were the first two generations.)

It looks to us as if Nokia could be the leader for a while. Ollila is doing all the right things.

A Successful Lady's View

No one does the differentiating thing in magazines better than Tina Brown. When she was at *Vanity Fair*, she pushed celebrity journals to the limit. She created a big stir at the staid *New Yorker*. Critics and fans alike admit that she can make a splash and draw attention to her products.

Now she's on to a new magazine called *Talk*, and she already has people talking about her new magazine.

But what we were struck with was her five lessons on marketing that were reported in *The Wall Street Journal:*

1. Trust your instincts. I will listen to anybody. . . . But I usually come to my senses and try to get back in touch with what I initially thought.

   (She does her own strategy.)

2. Have a strong visual identity. . . . Doing bits and pieces of everybody else . . . isn't going to help you.

(Your product should be different.)

3. Throw a party. A launch needs all the help it can get. It is a big country. You have to reach a lot of people.

(You have to differentiate in the mind.)

4. Be creative with spending. Find new talent and package your product in a different way. If you don't have a (large) budget, you have to have a point of view.

(Once again, be different.)

5. Utilize your existing talent in different ways. With writers, for instance . . . the trick is finding what turns them on . . . making them feel they can write about topics they couldn't before.[2]

(One more time, be different.)

Here's a very successful lady who is obviously in charge of strategy and a strong believer in being different. Not bad thinking for a magazine editor. She gets it.

In 1966, Peter Drucker defined leadership when he wrote: "The foundation of effective leadership is thinking through the organization's mission, defining it and establishing it, clearly and visibly."

Well, we're now in a new millennium and an age of killer competition. We would change only one word in that definition to bring it up to date: "The foundation of effective leadership is thinking through the organization's *difference*, defining it and establishing it, clearly and visibly."

Rosser Reeves would have agreed with that revision.

NOTES

Chapter 1   The Tyranny of Choice

1. Federal Reserve Bank of Dallas, 1998 annual report, pp. 4–6.
2. Interview with the authors, March 29, 1999.

Chapter 2   Whatever Happened to the U.S.P.?

1. Rosser Reeves, *Reality in Advertising* (Knopf, 1960), pp. 47–48.
2. "Creative Differences," *Advertising Age* (November 17, 1997): 1.

Chapter 3   Reinventing the U.S.P.

1. Interview with the authors, March 19, 1999.
2. Tara Parker-Pope, "Stopping Diaper Leaks Can Be Nasty Business, P&G Shows Its Rivals," *The Wall Street Journal* (April 5, 1999).
3. "Differentiation or Salience," *Journal of Advertising Research* (November–December 1997): 7–14.
4. Robert McMath, *What Were They Thinking?* (Times Business, 1998), p. 86.
5. "Differentiation or Salience," op. cit.

Chapter 4   Quality and Customer Orientation Are Rarely Differentiating Ideas

1. Jan Berry, "Consumers Keep the Upper Hand," *American Demographics* (September 1998).
2. Christopher W. Hart and Michael D. Johnson, *Marketing Management* (spring 1999).
3. Leonard Berry and A. Parasuramy, *Marketing Services* (New York: Free Press, 1991), p. 137.
4. "The Return of Michael Porter," *Fortune* (February 1, 1999): 135–137.

Chapter 5   Creativity Is Not a Differentiating Idea

1. "Ad Accountability," *Advertising Age* (March 22, 1999): 26.
2. "Speakers at Four A's Meeting Urge Agencies to Meet Competition from Management Consultants," *The New York Times* (April 26, 1999).
3. Interview with the authors, March 29, 1999.
4. Sergio Zyman, *The End of Marketing As We Know It* (Harper Business, 1999).

Chapter 6   Price Is Rarely a Differentiating Idea

1. David Ogilvy, "Fiftieth Anniversary Luncheon Speech," Advertising Research Foundation, New York City, March 18, 1986.
2. "Siberian Soft-Drink Queen Outmarkets Coke and Pepsi," *The Wall Street Journal* (August 23, 1999).
3. David Cowan, "Free For All," *The Wall Street Journal* (July 28, 1999).

Chapter 9   Differentiation Takes Place in the Mind

1. The *Journal of Consumer Marketing*,
2. "The Logic of Product Line Extension," *Harvard Business Review* (November–December 1994).

Chapter 10   Being First Is a Differentiating Idea

1. Frank Sulloway, *Bound to Rebel* (Vintage Books, 1997).
2. "A New Brand of Bottled Water with a Twist," *The New York Times* (June 3, 1999): C10.

Chapter 12   Leadership Is a Way to Differentiate

1. Hans and Michael Eysenck, *Mindwatching* (Anchor Press—Doubleday, 1983).
2. "Ads Hit Target," *USA Today* (January 15, 1996): 6B.

Chapter 13   Heritage Is a Differentiating Idea

1. Interview with the authors, March 29, 1999.
2. Ted Anthony, "In a Dizzying Market, America's Oldest Brands Court Continued Prosperity," *Associated Press Newswires* (March 22, 1999).
3. Ibid.
4. "DDB Worldwide Hopes to Build on the Legacy of 50 Years of Industry Innovation," *The New York Times* (June 1, 1999): C12.
5. "The Beauty of Global," *Business Week* (June 28, 1999): 70.
6. David Yale, *The New York Times* (July 14, 1999).

Chapter 14 Market Specialty Is a Differentiating Idea

1. Robert Kiener, "Hitting on All Cylinders," *Nation's Business* (June 1999): 57–58.

Chapter 15 Preference Is a Differentiating Idea

1. Robert Cialdini, "Influence: The Psychology of Persuasion" (William Morrow, 1993).
2. Randy Cohen, "Madison Avenue Medicine," *The New York Times Magazine* (June 27, 1999): 20.
3. Stanley Resor, "The Spirit of Emulation," *Printer's Ink* (April 1929).

Chapter 17 Being the Latest Can Be a Differentiating Idea

1. Clayton Christensen, *The Innovator's Dilemma: When New Technologies Cause Great Firms to Fail.*
2. "Nothing But Net," *Business Week* (August 2, 1999): 72.

Chapter 18 Hotness Is a Way to Differentiate

1. "Critics Agree," *The New York Times* (March 15, 1999): C14.
2. "The Future of Public Relations Is on the Internet," *Public Relations Strategist* (spring 1999): 7–10.

Chapter 19 Growth Can Destroy Differentiation

1. "Starbucks Holders Wake Up, Smell the Coffee, and Sell," *The Wall Street Journal* (July 2, 1999): B3.

Chapter 21   Being Different in Different Places

1. "How McDonald's Tailors Its Brand Identity to Local Markets," *Campaign* (August 1997): 29.
2. "Brewing a Worldly Brand," *Andersen Consulting Outlook* (June 1999).
3. Bhavna Mistry, "On a Global Mission," *Marketing Event* (October 9, 1997): 41.

Chapter 22   Maintaining Your Difference

1. *Fortune* (September 20, 1999): 220.

Chapter 23   Who Is in Charge of Differentiation?

1. "Why CEOs Fail," *Fortune* (June 21, 1999): 69.
2. "Finding the Seduction Point," *The Wall Street Journal* (July 26, 1999): 1.

INDEX

ABB (Asea Brown Boveri), 147
ABC, 5
Absolut vodka, 55, 122
AccuRay, 147
Advertising:
 agencies, corporate ego, 209
 budgets of big companies, 71–72
 creativity in, 37–44
 statistics (TV commercials), 74–75
 unique selling propositions (U.S.P.),
  11–17
 vagueness in, 37–39
Advertising Age, 39
Advil, 15, 85–86
Aetna/US Healthcare, 3
Airborne, 90–91
Air-conditioning, 90
Airlines, 30–31, 34–35, 46–47, 68–69,
 136, 199
Airports (early 1970s *vs.* late 1990s), 6
Allen, Robert, 206
Alpert, Hershel, 63
Alperts Furniture Showplace (Rhode
 Island), 62–63
Alpo, 190
Amazon.com, 61, 92, 201
American Advertising Federation, 39
American Airlines, 30–31
American Animal Hospital Association,
 137
American Association of Advertising
 Agencies, 39
American Express, 99
American's Health Network, 134
American Society for Quality Control, 29
Americare, 3
AmericasDoctor.com Inc., 134
Ames, 100, 196
Amphicar, 182
Amstel Light, 181
Amusement parks (early 1970s *vs.* late
 1990s), 6

Anacin, 20
Anheuser-Busch, 203
Animal crackers, 154
Antarctica beer, 109
Antonini, Joseph, 206
Apple Computer, 207
 Newton, 77, 183, 207
Argentina, 102, 121–122
Armani, 189
Armstrong tires, 3
Aron Streit Inc., 151
Asea Brown Boveri (ABB), 147
Aston Martin, 3
Athletes, endorsements by, 141, 142, 143
AT&T, 38, 49, 182, 206
Attribute(s), 95–105, 185, 192
 being green, 104–105
 bloodless surgery, 103
 cars, 97, 98, 102
 credit cards, 99
 culture and, 192
 definition, 95
 fast food, 100–101, 102
 focus as key, 97
 Massachusetts Museum of
  Contemporary Art, 103–104
 negative, 102–103
 opposite, 96
 owning, 96
 razors, 98–99
 relative importance of, 97
 retailing, 97, 99–100
 sacrificing, 185
 simplicity, 104
 toothpaste, 95–96
 water, low sodium in Argentina, 102
Australia, 121
Automobiles, 3
 American Motors, 3, 8
 Amphicar, 182
 attribute ownership, 97, 98, 102
 BMW, 3, 15, 50, 98, 102, 174

Automobiles *(Continued)*
  Cadillac, 55, 132, 146, 165, 197
  Chevrolet, 5, 8, 80, 98, 132, 181
  Chrysler, 3, 84, 112, 132, 196
  Corvette, 185
  Dodge, 132
  Edsel, 42
  Ferrari, 3, 98, 183
  Ford, 3, 5, 8, 112, 131, 132, 174
  General Motors, 3, 71, 112, 146, 170,
    196, 207
  Hemmings Motor News, 130–131
  high-priced cars, 54–55
  Hyundai, 3
  idea that failed (visionary drivetrain),
    89
  Isuzu, 3
  Jaguar, 98
  J.D. Powers, 136, 140, 166
  Lamborghini, 3
  law of division, 5
  Lincoln, 110–111, 165–166
  Mercedes, 3, 49, 98, 132, 140
  Mercedes-Benz, 55, 102
  Mercury, 98
  Mitsubishi, 3
  Nissan, 3, 98
  Oldsmobile, 98
  Plymouth, 5
  Pontiac, 68
  Porsche, 170, 181, 185
  Renault, 3
  Rolls-Royce, 131, 197, 202
  styles/models (early 1970s *vs.* late
    1990s), 6
  Subaru, 133, 142, 185
  Toyota, 3, 8, 98, 110
  Volkswagen, 3, 40, 79, 98, 132, 206
  Volvo, 3, 24, 77, 98, 172, 173, 174,
    185
  Yugo, 121
Auto Zone, 58
Avis, 40, 66, 69
Axid, 158

Babies "R" Us, 58
Baby Superstore, 58
Baci, 189
Ballpoint pens, 87
Banana Republic, 129
Band-Aid, 86
Banking, 27–28, 66, 69–70, 183–184
Bank of America, 119
Bank One, 162
Barnum's Animals (Nabisco), 154
Barron's guides, 140

Bass Pro Shop, 2
Batesville caskets, 76, 153–154
Becker beer, 137, 138
Beef spokespersons, 142
Beer, 87, 109, 112, 117, 137–138, 172,
    180–181, 185, 191, 192–193, 200, 203
Belgium, water, 101
Benetton, 129
Bentley, 3
Bernbach, Bill, 40, 41, 51, 119, 120
Berry, Leonard, 31
Bic pens, 87
Black & Decker, 149
Blockbuster Video, 129
Bloodless surgery, 103
Blue Cross, 3
B. Manischewitz, 151
BMW, 3, 15, 50, 98, 102, 174
Boeing, 88, 197–198
Book titles, new (early 1970s *vs.* late
    1990s), 6
Bose Wave radio, 24–25
Bottled water brands (early 1970s *vs.* late
    1990s), 6
Brahma beer, 109
Brand graveyard, 8
Brand name becoming generic, 81, 86,
    131, 148
Brand science (Young & Rubicam), 13
Braun, 91
Brazil (beer), 109
Breadth-of-line differentiation, 57–63
    becoming more shopper friendly, 59–60
    line extensions, 79–80, 170–171, 200,
    202
    problems, 59
    on the Web, 60–61
Breakfast cereals (early 1970s *vs.* late
    1990s), 6
Bridgestone tires, 3
Brigadeiro, 190
Brigg umbrella, 137
Brite Tip, 147–148
British Air, 68
Brooks Sports, 141
Brown, Tina, 211–212
Bru, 101
Budweiser, 112, 117, 180
Buitoni, 189
Burberry, 189
Burger King, 100–101, 139, 185–186, 197,
    198–199
Burnett, Leo, 190
Bush, George W., 118
Business Travel News, 144
Business Week, 167

Cabela's, 2
Cadillac, 55, 132, 146, 165, 197
Caldor, 100
California, public healthcare report card, 4
Camel cigarettes, 141
Cameras, 86, 87
Campeau, 129
Campsa, 174–176
Car(s). *See* Automobiles
Carnation, 189
Carrier, 90
Carrier, Willis, 90
Carrots, 46
Caskets, 76, 153–154
Category killers (superstores), 57–58
Category ownership, 108
CBS, 5
Celebrity endorsements, 141–142, 143
Cellophane tape, 86, 131
CEOs. *See* Leadership/management
Chanel, 142, 189
Charles Schwab brokerage, 48, 138, 162
Charlie the Tuna, 125
Charmin, 80, 132
Chase bank, 27
Chase & Sanborn coffee, 52
Chevrolet, 5, 8, 80, 98, 132, 181
Chicken, 6, 17, 24–25, 125, 165, 185, 192
Chick-Fil-A, 24, 165
China, 4, 115, 143, 190, 193
Chipotle Mexican grill, 184
Chiquita bananas, 17
Choice, 1–9, 57
  caveat to business, 8
  China, 4
  dead brands, 8
  emerging nations, 4–5
  explosion of (table of items, early 1970s *vs.* late 1990s), 6
  fishing gear, 2
  healthcare, 3–4
  law of division, 5
  prediction, 9
  restaurants, 2
  SKUs, statistics, 2–3
  tyranny of, 7–8
Choice industry (guides), 7
Chrysler, 3, 84, 112, 132, 196
Chupa Chups, 113
Church's Chicken, 24, 165
Cialdini, Robert, 135
Cigarette(s), 88–89, 112, 141, 143, 180
  smokeless, 88–89
Cigna, 3
Circuit City, 196

Classic Sports, 171
Coca-Cola, 41, 42–43, 52–53, 69, 79, 85, 86, 96, 97, 100, 108, 120, 171, 174, 192
Coffee, 52, 188
Cognac, 143
Cohen, Randy, 140
Coke. *See* Coca-Cola
Colgate, 6, 19, 22, 112, 201
Colleges, 68, 84, 140
Columbia health care, 3
Columbia Savings, 27
Commerce bank, 27
Commodities, differentiating, 17, 25–26
Communications program, and resources for, 70
Community colleges (early 1970s *vs.* late 1990s), 6
Compaq Computer, 8, 47, 48, 89, 160
Competition, analyzing/tearing apart, 22–23
CompUSA, 58
Computers:
  Compaq Computer, 8, 47, 48, 89, 160
  CompUSA, 58
  Dell Computer, 47–48
  Digital Equipment Corporation (DEC), 8, 160, 162, 207, 208
  hard-as-nails (Iron Computer), 72
  law of division, 5
  PC models (early 1970s *vs.* late 1990s), 6
  U.S. advantage, 120
  used in competitive analysis, 22–23
  Xerox, 79
Condé Naste Traveler magazine, 136, 144
Consumer items, early 1970s and late 1990s (proliferation of choices), 6
Consumer Reports, 7
Consumers Digest, 7
Contact lens types (early 1970s *vs.* late 1990s), 6
Contadina, 190
Contrary, staying, 196–197
Convergence, 182–184
  in banking, 183–184
  disasters, 182–183
  why it doesn't work, 183
Convertoplane, 182
Cooper tires, 3
Corbett Canyon (wine), 164–165
Cordis, 147
Cordovan tires, 3
Corona beer, 185, 192–193
Cortopassi, Dino, 149, 150, 152
Corvette, 185

Cosmetics, 123
Costco, 47
Cowan, David, 54
Cox, Box, 27
Craftsman tools, 196
Crain, Rance, 39
Cray supercomputers, 111
Creativity in advertising, 37–44
Creativity *vs.* logic, 66
Credit cards, 88, 99
Crest toothpaste, 19, 96, 112, 146, 185,
    200–201
Cristal, 137
Cross pens, 117
Customer satisfaction, 29–30, 33

Daewoo, 177
Daihatsu, 3
Daiwa, 3
Dannon yogurt, 128, 193
Dayton Hudson, 100
Dayton tires, 3
DDB Worldwide Communications,
    119–120
Dead brands (proliferation of choices), 8
DEC. *See* Digital Equipment Corporation
    (DEC)
de Havilland (British aircraft maker),
    88
Dell, Michael, 197
Dell Computers, 47–48, 159–160, 185,
    197
Del Monte, 151, 152
Dental flosses (early 1970s *vs.* late 1990s),
    6
Diaper wars, 20, 21
DieHard batteries, 196
Dietary supplement (Airborne), 90–91
Difference, maintaining your, 195–203
    evolving/adjusting your difference,
        200–202
    maintaining consistency, 198–199
    remembering your difference, 195–196
    staying connected, 200
    staying contrary, 196–198
    tinkering *vs.* evolving, 202–203
Differentiating ideas:
    attribute ownership, 95–105
    being first, 83–93
    being latest, 155–162
    heritage, 115–125
    hotness, 163–168
    how product made, 145–154
    market leadership, 107–113
    market specialty, 127–134
    preference, 135–144

Differentiating ideas that rarely/don't
    work:
    breadth of line, 57–63
    creativity in advertising, 37–44
    price, 45–55
    quality and customer orientation,
        27–35
Differentiation:
    caution flags, 26
    of commodities, 17, 25–26
    global issues, 187–194
    and growth, 169–177
    importance as strategy, 25
    leadership/management, 205–212
    locational, 187–194
    maintaining, 195–203
    in the mind (*see* Psychology of
        differentiation)
    of product, 23
    for psychological types (four categories),
        14–15
    requiring sacrifice, 179–186
    unique selling proposition (U.S.P.),
        11–17, 19–26
Differentiation, steps to, 65–72
    logic *vs.* creativity, 66
    power of logic, 65–66
    step 1: making sense in context, 67
    step 2: finding differentiating idea,
        67–68
    step 3: having credentials, 68–69
    step 4: communicating difference,
        69–70
DiGiorno Pizza, 148
Digital Equipment Corporation (DEC), 8,
    160, 162, 207, 208
Digital Gold Rush, 61
Digital Island, 167–168
Digital Research, 87
Diners Club, 88
Discount brokerage (Charles Schwab), 48,
    138, 162
Discounters, 58–59
Disney, 189, 199
Disruptive technologies, 161–162
Dodge, 132
Dole pineapple, 17
Domino's pizza, 81, 93
Dove soap, 148
Dow Chemical, 161
Dreyer, William, 111
Dreyer's ice cream, 111–112
Drkoop.com Inc., 134
Drucker, Peter, 208, 212
Drug industry, 6, 15, 20, 85–86, 136,
    157–158, 200

battle over acid stomachs, 157–158
number of OTC pain relievers (early
    1970s *vs.* late 1990s), 6
number of prescription drugs (early
    1970s *vs.* late 1990s), 6
Dunlap, Al, 206
Dunlop tires, 3
Duracell, 112, 130, 181, 185
Duxiana, 50
Dynastar, 148

ECO de los Andes, 102
Edison, Thomas, 93
Edsel, 42
Edy, Joseph, 111
Edy's ice cream, 111–112
Ehrich, Terry, 131
Einstein, Albert, 76
Electronic cameras, 162
Emerging nations (proliferation of
    choices), 4–5
Emery AirFreight, 179
Emotion and choice, 41–42
Employee motivation, 70
Englewood (New Jersey) Hospital and
    Medical Center, 103
Enrich bulb, 156
ENSR, 130
Environmental issues, 92, 104–105, 130
ESPN, 171
Ethics, and preference marketing, 140–141
eToys, Inc., 60, 201
Eveready, 130, 181
Eversharp, 87
Evian, 84
Excel, 200, 210
Expert:
    becoming, as differentiator, 130
    definition of, 127
Extending line. *See* Line extensions
Eysenck, Hans and Michael, 107

Family business, 123–124
Fast food:
    attributes in, 100–101
    Burger King/Whopper, 100–101, 139,
        185–186, 197, 198–199
    McDonald's, 6, 100–101, 102, 139, 151,
        171, 184, 186, 190–191, 192, 197,
        199, 203, 207
    pizza, 81, 93–148, 150, 184, 203, 207,
        210
    square hamburgers, 150–151
    White Castle, 150–151, 185
Fedders, 90
Federal Express (FedEx), 81, 86, 179, 186

Ferrari, 3, 98, 183
Fiat, 3
Fiberglas, 86
Financial Net News, 138
Finland, 188
Firestone tires, 3
First, being, 78, 83–93
    borrowed idea (example), 93
    environmental cause, profits to, 92
    firsts that are still firsts (examples), 84
    gardening (example), 91–92
    generic advantage, 86
    ignored advantage (example), 90
    importance of idea, 88, 89
    importance of staying first, 85
    no guarantee of success, 87–88
    power of, 78
    slow-to-catch-on (examples), 86–87
First Union National Bank, 183–184
Fishing gear (proliferation of choices), 2
Foot Locker, 49, 129, 185
Forbes, 167
Ford Motor Company, 3, 5, 8, 112, 131,
    132, 174
Formica, 86
Formula One racing tire, 183
Fortune magazine, 167
Four Seasons hotels, 143–144
Fox Sports, 171
Foxy lettuce package, 17
France, 121
Franzia, Teresa, 119
Franzia wine, 119
Free offers, 53–54, 71
French's mustard, 128
Fresh Samantha, 152
Friedman, Milton, 169
Frito-Lay chip varieties (early 1970s *vs.*
    late 1990s), 6
Frosty Paws (ice cream for dogs), 89
Fruit juice, 152

Galbraith, John Kenneth, 79
Gallo, Ernest, 119
Gallup survey, 29
Gap, The, 129
Garden.com, 91–92
Garden Ridge, 59
Gartner Group, 166
Gates, Bill, 210
Gatorade, 131
General Electric, 8, 16, 38, 127–128, 156,
    210
    blenders, 78
    GE-Godrej, 192
    jet engines, 197–198

General Foods, 52, 188
General Motors (GM), 3, 71, 112, 146, 170, 196, 207
General Tires, 3
Generic, brand name becoming, 81, 86, 131, 148
Germany, 121
Gevalia coffee, 188
Gillette, 23–24, 88, 98–99, 156, 174
Giovanni, A.P., 119
Glassman, Richard, 91
Glenlivit Distillery, 117
Glieck, James, 9
Global marketing. *See* Marketing, global
GM. *See* General Motors (GM)
Goizueta, Robert, 171
Goodrich, 8
Goodyear, 3, 8
GoreTex, 54, 86
Granite Rock Company (California), 149
Greenbrier hotel (West Virginia), 120
Green Giant, 17
Grey Poupon mustard, 55
Growth, 169–177, 180–181, 195
    damaging your difference, 172, 180–181
    distraction, 170
    Korean disaster (Daewoo), 177
    less can be more, 173–174
    line extensions, 79–80, 170–171, 200, 202 (*see also* Breadth-of-line differentiation)
    by multiple brands, 174–176
    Spanish multibrand story (Repsol), 174–176

Hahn, Carl, 206
Hall Flying Car (1945), 182
Halo effect, 97
Hamburger wars, 139. *See also* Fast food
Handcrafted, 153
Haomen Brewery, Beijing, 143
Harvard, 84
Healthcare (proliferation of choices), 3–4
Health sites on Internet, 133–134
Heineken beer, 137, 181, 191
Heinz, 108, 132, 151, 152
Hellenic Institute of Marketing in Greece, 188
Hellmann's mayonnaise, 128
Hemmings Motor News, 130–131
Heritage (as differentiating idea), 78, 115–125
    anticompetitor, 122–123
    bringing forward, 117–118
    of a character, 125
    doubling back on, 119–120

family business, 123–125
French success, 123
locational, 120–121
in politics and law, 118
psychology of, 116
substitute for leadership, 116–117
updating, 120
Hershey's, 108
Herta, 190
Hertz, 16, 40, 69, 84, 109–110, 112
Hewlett-Packard, 84
Higgins, Ron, 167–168
Hillsdale College, Michigan, 68
Hills department stores, 129
History Channel, 171
Hollywood, 166
Home Depot, 58, 59, 60, 196
Honda, 3, 8, 98
Hôtel Hermitage (Monte Carlo), 120
Hotness strategy, 163–168
    chicken, 165
    Corbett Canyon wine, 164–165
    Digital Island, 167–168
    executing a shift, 164–165
    Fortune magazine, 167
    industry experts, 166
    industry ratings, 166
    lying about being "hot," 165–166
    press, 167
    sales, 166
    ways to be "hot," 166
Houston TV channels (early 1970s *vs.* late 1990s), 6
How a product is made. *See* Product design/process as differentiating idea
Hughes Electronics, 89
Huish Detergents Inc., 123
Hunt-Wesson, 23
Hydrox, 88
Hyundai, 3

IBM, 47, 66, 68, 87, 108, 210
Ibuprofen, 85–86
India, 191–192, 193
Information:
    in advertising, 43–44
    statistics on overcommunication of, 74
Intel, 20, 156
InteliHealth Inc., 134
Internet:
    access problems, 168
    Amazon.com, 61, 92, 201
    and convergence, 182
    Digital Island, 167–168
    electronic bombardment, 74–75
    free offerings on, 53–54

Garden.com, 91–92
guidance needed, 62
health sites, 133–134
pet sites, 58, 136, 137
proliferation of choices, 6, 7, 9
shopping, 60–61
site-eat-site world, 61
Starbucks, 173
toys, 201
Web sites (early 1970s *vs.* late 1990s), 6
Wingspan.com, 162
Interstate Department Stores, 129
IntraNetics, 104
Iron Computer, 72
Isuzu, 3
Italy, 121

Jack Daniel's bourbon, 96
Jaguar, 98
Japan, 115, 121, 168, 193
J.D. Powers, 136, 140, 166
Jeep, 132
Jell-O, 86
Jim Beam bourbon, 96
Johnson & Johnson, 147
Jolly Green Giant, 125
Jolly Time, 54
Joy perfume, 54
J.P. Morgan, 38
Jumbo Sports, 53
Just for Feet, 53
J. Walter Thompson Co. advertising, 141

Kaiser, 3
Keeper Springs Mountain Spring Water, 92
Kelleher, Herb, 46, 199, 210
Kellogg's, 193, 206
Kelly tires, 3
Kenmore, 196
Kennedy, Brian, 110
Kentucky Fried Chicken (KFC), 6, 24,
  165, 185, 192
  Colonel Sanders character, 125, 165
  menu items (early 1970s *vs.* late 1990s),
    6
Kia, 3
Kimberly-Clark, 21
KitchenAid, 128
Kit Kat, 189
Kleenex, 86
Kleisner, Ted, 120
Kmart, 47, 53, 58, 196, 206
Kodak, 86, 162
Koop, Dr. C. Everett, 134
Korea/North Korea, 5, 177
Kraft, 128–129

Kranson Industries, 91
Krazy Glue, 86

Lamborghini, 3
Langbo, Arnold, 206
Lange, 156–157
Lasky, Michael, 21
Latest. *See* Product(s), latest (next
  generation)
Law of division (proliferation of choices),
  5
Lawn mower, ultimate, 153
Lazarus, Charles, 57
Lazarus, Richard and Bernice, 42
Lazarus, Shelly, 39–40, 42
Leadership, market. *See* Market leadership
Leadership/management, 205–212
  CEO failures, list of (*Fortune* magazine),
    205–206
  CEO hobby, 132
  CEO involvement, 208–209
  CEO leading in strategy, 210
  CEO personal agenda, 208
  CEO success, example of (Manzi),
    209–210
  corporate ego, 209
  Drucker's definition of, 212
  strategy *vs.* execution, 205–206,
    207–208
Learning, 76
Lechters, 58
Leica, 87
Lenzing, 111
Levi Strauss, 6, 61, 189
Levitt, Theodore, 16, 25–26, 187
Levy's Jewish rye bread, 41
Lexus, 136, 140
Lifebuoy soap, 19
Limited, The, 129
Lincoln automobile, 110–111, 165–166
Line extensions, 79–80, 170–171, 200,
  202. *See also* Breadth-of-line
  differentiation
Listerine, 77, 102
L.J. Hooker, 129
L.L. Bean, 2, 117
Locke lawn mower, 153
Logic, 65–66, 77
Lollipops, 113
L'Oréal, 123
Lotus Development Corporation, 67, 200,
  209–210
Louis Vuitton, 189
Lucky Strike, 141
Lutz, Bob, 196
Lux, 141, 193

Mackintosh (Nestle), 190
Macy's department stores, 129
Magazine titles (early 1970s vs. late
    1990s), 6
Maggi, 189
Magic ingredient, 146
Magna International, 132
Maker's Mark, 96
Malaysia, 153
Malcolm Baldrige National Quality
    Award, 32
Manzi, Jim, 209–210
Market, virgin, 32
Marketing:
    advertising (see Advertising)
    differentiation in (see Differentiation)
    expense/budget, 70, 71–72
    one of fathers of (Levitt), 25
    price promotions, 50–51 (see also Price)
Marketing, global, 187–194
    culture, 115
    Domino's home delivery idea in Madrid,
        93
    emerging nations (proliferation of
        choices), 4–5
    example (Heineken), 191
    locational heritage (list of countries),
        121
    rules, 192–193
    universals, 189
    varying preferences, 194
Market Intelligence Service Ltd., 20
Market leadership, 107–113, 116–117
    category ownership, 108
    don't be afraid to brag, 108–109
    forms of, 110–111
    heritage a substitute for, 116–117
    performance leadership, 111
    platform, 111–112
    psychology of leadership, 107–108
    sales leadership, 110
    strength of, 112–113
    technology leadership, 111
Market leadership examples:
    beer in Brazil, 109
    Hertz, 109–110
    lollipops, 113
Market specialist(s), 81, 127–134
    brand name becoming generic, 131
    environmental due diligence as
        differentiator, 130
    expertise as differentiator, 130
    vs. generalist, 127–128
    positioning yourself as, 132–133
    power of specialist, 81, 130
    publishing, 130–131

retailers, 129
    staying specialized, 131–132
    surplus of, 133
Marlboro, 112, 143, 180
Martell Noblige, 143
Massachusetts Museum of Contemporary
    Art, 103–104
MasterCard, 99
Matzo company, 151
Maybelline, 123
Mazda, 3
McCoy, John B., 162
McDonald's, 6, 100–101, 102, 139, 151,
    171, 184, 186, 190–191, 192, 197,
    199, 203, 207
MCI, 49
McIlhenny, Paul C.P., 118
McKinsey, 189
McMath, Robert, 22
Meats/produce, differentiating, 17
Medicare/Medicaid, 3
Mediconsult.com Inc., 134
Medipren, 85
MedPartners, 3
Medscan Inc., 133
Mennen's vitamin E deodorant, 77
Mercedes, 3, 49, 98, 132, 140
Mercedes-Benz, 55, 102
Mercury, 98
Merit, 174
Merrill Lynch, 48, 162
Mexico, 192–193
Michelin tires, 3
Michelob beer, 172, 180–181
Microsoft, 87, 170, 200, 209, 210
Microwave ovens, 86, 158–159
Midwest Express Airlines, 34–35, 136
Mighty Dog, 189
Milacron, 111
Milestone Scientific, 159
Milk, 6, 142
Miller beer, 180
Minds. See Psychology of differentiation
Miracle-Gro, 15
Mitsubishi, 3
Mobil, 174
Money magazine, 138
Monoseal, 153
Moog, Dr. Carol, 7, 42, 116
Motrin, 85, 86
Mouthwashes (early 1970s vs. late 1990s),
    6
Movie releases (early 1970s vs. late 1990s),
    6
Multi-Mile tires, 3
Multiplan (healthcare), 3

Multiscan, 121–122
Museums, 103–104

Nabisco (National Biscuit), 88, 154, 171
NBC, 5
Nescafé, 193
Nestlé, 189, 193
Nestlé, Henri, 189
New Coke, 42. *See also* Coca-Cola
New products. *See* Product(s), new
Newsweek, 84
Newton, 77, 183, 207
New Yorker, 211
New York Times, 139, 167
New Zealand, 121
Next generation. *See* Product(s), latest
  (next generation)
Nike, 49, 136, 141, 142, 172, 174
Nintendo, 87
Nissan, 3, 98
Nokia, 210–211
Noodle Kidoodle, 58
Nordstrom, 32, 33, 67, 185
Nordstrom, William E., 33
NorthFace (outdoor jacket), 54
Nuprin, 85

Obsolete, making yourself, 156
Ogilvy, David, 51–52, 140
Oil of Olay, 189
Okidata's Doc-it, 182
Oldsmobile, 98
Ollila, Jorma, 210–211
On Health Network Co., 134
Operational effectiveness *vs.* strategic
  positioning, 33–34
Opincar, John, 72
Oral-B toothbrushes, 23
Oreo cookies, 88
Orvis, 2
Otis Elevator, 16
Overcommunication, 74
Owen-Jones, CEO (L'Oréal), 123
Oxford healthcare, 3

PacifiCare, 4
Packaging distributors, 91
Palmer, Robert, 207, 208
Palm Pilot, 77
Pampero (Venezuelan ketchup), 151
Papa John's Pizza, 150, 210
Party City, 59
Patent protection, 21–22, 146, 147
Paulig coffee, 188
PC. *See* Computers
PC Magazine, 138

PC World, 138
PDA, 182
Penthouse magazine, 84
Pentium, 156. *See also* Intel
People magazine, 84
Pepcid, 158
Pepsi, 41, 52–53, 85, 86, 96, 97, 100, 185,
  197, 203, 207
Performance leadership, 111
Perrier, 189
Personal agenda, CEOs, 208, 210
Personal computers. *See* Computers
Pet products, 58, 136–137
Petronor, 174
Pets.com, 136
Petsmart.com, 58, 136
Petstore.com, 136, 137
Pewter, handcrafted, 153
Philadelphia brand cream cheese, 129
Philip Morris, 52, 71, 180
Pimenova, Victoria, 52–53
Pioneers in categories, still leaders, 84
Pirelli tires, 3
Pizza, 81, 93–148, 150, 184, 203, 207,
  210
Pizza Hut, 81
Planters' Mr. Peanut, 125
Playboy magazine, 84
Plymouth, 5
Polo brand, 172
Pond's cold cream, 141
Pontiac, 68
Pony Express, 117
Popcorn, 23, 54
Popeyes Chicken, 24, 165
Pop-Tarts, varieties of (early 1970s *vs.* late
  1990s), 6
Pork ("the other white meat"), 17
Porsche, 170, 181, 185
Porter, Michael, 33–34, 45, 46
Positioning, 33–34
  competition, repositioning, 102
  definition, 73
  as specialist, 132–133
  strategic, *vs.* operational effectiveness,
    33–34
Pratt & Whitney, 197
Preference marketing, 135–144
  beer in Chile, 137–138
  celebrity endorsements, 141–142
  China (cognac/heroes), 143
  hotels, 143–144
  legitimate, 140
  and professional ethics, 140–141
  questionable, 139
  rain in Britain, 137

Preference marketing (*Continued*)
  Schwab, 138–139 (*see also* Schwab,
    Charles)
  sneakers, 141
  social proof, 136–137
  spirit of emulation, 141–142
Prell shampoo, 203
Premier cigarettes, 88–89
Prestige, and high price, 54
Price, 45–55
  building price advantage, 46–47
  differentiating with high price, 54–55
  free offerings, 53–54, 71
  getting around, 48–50
  tried and true methods (list), 49–50
Prilosec, 158
Principle of social proof, 135–137
Procter & Gamble, 21, 71, 122, 123,
  200
Product(s), latest (next generation),
    155–162
  adding another technology, 159–160
  breaking with the past, 158–159
  Dell Computer, 159–160
  drug industry (battle over acid
    stomachs), 157–158
  latest can sneak up on you, 161–162
  latest doesn't always work, 160–161
  latest should be different, 162
  making yourself obsolete, 156
  microwave ovens, 158–159
  ski boot saga, 156–157
  taking advantage of history, 160
Product(s), new, 20
  in 1987 *vs.* 1998, 20, 21
Product advertising, informative, 43–44.
    See also Advertising
Product design/process as differentiating
    idea, 145–154
  animal crackers, 154
  caskets, 153–154
  dramatizing difference, 147–148
  giving up old way, 151–152
  high-tech ingredients, 146–147
  magic ingredient, 146
  making it the old-fashioned way, 151
  making it the right way, 149–150
  pewter handmade in Malaysia, 153
  pizza, 150
  product innovation, 148
  square hamburgers, 150–151
  system innovation, 148–149
Product sacrifice, 184–185
Promotions, price, 50–51
Prucare, 3
Psychology, leadership, 107–108

Psychology of differentiation, 14–15,
    41–42, 73–81
  buying what others buy, 78–79
  changing; minds not, 79, 83, 172, 184
  confusion; minds hating, 76
  electronic bombardment, 74–75
  emotion and choice, 41–42
  focus; minds losing, 79–80
  insecurity of minds, 77–78, 115
  limits of the mind, 75–76
  line extensions, some surprising
    research, 80
  overcommunication; minds not coping
    with, 74
  risk, five forms of perceived, 78–79
  simplicity, power of, 77
  specialist, power of, 81
Psychology of problem-solving/decision-
    making (four types), 14–15
  feelers, 15
  intuitives, 15
  sensors, 16
  thinkers, 15
Publications, niche, 141
Public relations, 71, 167, 168
Pujals, Fernandez, 93

Q-tips, 86
Quality, 27–35
  differentiating with high price, 54–55
  tools for, 28
  war on, 28
Quality Institute International Inc., 33
Quinlan, Michael, 207
Quorum (healthcare), 3

Radio stations (early 1970s *vs.* late 1990s),
  6
Ralph Lauren, 172
Ray-O-Vac, 130
Razors, attributes in, 98–99
Redenbacher, Orville, 23, 54
Reebok, 192
Reeves, Rosser, 11, 14, 16, 19, 37, 40, 51,
  102, 212
Reinhard, Keith, 120
Renault, 3
Repsol (Spain's oil company), 174–176
Resor, Stanley, 141
Restaurant(s) (proliferation of choices), 2
Restaurant News, 166
Retailing:
  attributes, 97, 99–100
  Sears, 3, 196
  specialists, 129
  sports, 53

Reynolds, 87, 88–89
Rich's Frozen Foods, 124
Ricoh, 86
RisCasi & Davis law firm, 118
Risk, kinds of perceived, 78
Ritz-Carlton, 143–144
Roadhandler tires, 196
Rolex watches, 54
Rolls-Royce, 131, 197, 202
Roper Starch Worldwide, 28, 43
Rosen, Ben, 89
Rosen, Harold, 89
Rosen Motors, 89
Royal Selangor, 153
Runners World, 141
Running shoe styles (early 1970s *vs.* late 1990s), 6
Running Times, 141
Russian Crazy Cola, 52–53
Russian vodka, 120, 121, 122

Sacrifice, differentiation requiring, 179–186
    attribute sacrifice, 185
    feeling good about it, 185–186
    kinds of sacrifice, 184–185
    more is less, 179–180
    product sacrifice, 184–185
    target market sacrifice, 185
Sales leadership, 110
Sam's American Choice (competitor to Tide), 122–123
Saran Wrap, 86
Schnatter, John, 150, 210
Schultz, Howard, 173
Schwab, Charles, 48, 138, 162
Science Diet, 136
Scotch tape, 86, 131
Scott, 80, 86, 132
Sculley, John, 207
Seagram & Sons Inc., 143
Sears, 3, 196
Sentry tires, 3
7-Eleven, 176
Sharp copying machine, 86
Silicon Graphics, 111, 147, 170
Simplicity, power of, 77
"Site-eat-site" world, 61
Skiing equipment, 148, 156–157
SKUs, statistics (proliferation of choices), 2–3
Small Business Administration, 66
Smart Money, 138
Smuckers jelly, 128
SnackWell, 171
Sobel, Robert, 118

Social proof, principle of, 140
Soft drink brands (early 1970s *vs.* late 1990s), 6
Soft drink wars. *See* Coca-Cola; Pepsi
Software titles (early 1970s *vs.* late 1990s), 6
Solis, 190
Sony, 146, 182
Sotheby's auction house, 117
Southwest Airlines, 46–47, 199, 210
Spanish multibrand story, 174–176
Specialist. *See* Market specialist(s)
Sports Authority, 53, 58
Sports retailing, 53
Sprint, 49
Stanislaus Food Products, 149
Staples, 58, 129
Starbucks, 173
Starch research, 28, 43
Star-Kist tuna, 125
Steinway pianos, 117
Stempel, Robert, 207
Stewart, Martha, 210
Stolichnaya, 122
Strategy:
    and CEO, 210
    differentiation as, 25
    vs. execution, 205–206, 207–208
    strategic positioning *vs.* operational effectiveness, 33–34
Streit's Matzo, 151
Stronach, Frank, 132
Subaru, 133, 185
Subaru Outback, 142
Sulloway, Dr. Frank, 84–85
Summit Bank, 27–28
Sunbeam, 206
Sun Microsystems, 84
Sunrise coffee, 193
Sunshine Biscuits, 88
Superstores, 57–58
SUV styles (early 1970s *vs.* late 1990s), 6
Suzuki, 3
Swedish vodka, 122
Switzerland, 121
System innovation, 148–149

Tabasco sauce, 117–118
Tagamet, 158
Talk, 211
Target, 47, 58, 100, 196
Target market sacrifice, 185
Taylor Aerocar (1947), 182
Tear of the Clouds L.L.C., 92

Technology:
  adding another, 159–160
  disruptive, 161–162
  enabling competitive analysis, 22–23
  high-tech ingredients, 146–147
  leadership, 111
  and proliferation of choices, 9
Telephone answering machines, 87
Telephone rates, 49
TelePizza (Spain), 93
Television:
  proliferation of choice, 5
  screen sizes (early 1970s *vs.* late 1990s),
    6
  sports, 171
  statistics (TV commercials), 74–75
Texaco, 174
Texicana, 190
Third-party credentials, 167. *See also*
  Preference marketing
ThriveOnline, 134
Tide detergent (*vs.* Sam's American
  Choice), 122–123
Time magazine, 84
Tires, 3, 8, 183, 196
Tomato sauce, 149–150
Toothbrushes, 23–24
Toothpaste:
  attributes, 95–96
  Colgate, 6, 19, 112, 201
  Crest, 19, 96, 112, 146, 185, 200–201
Toyota, 3, 8, 98
Toyota Camry, 110
Toys "R" Us, 57, 58, 129, 201
Tradition, 161
Trane, 90
Trantolo & Trantolo law firm, 118
TricorBraun, 91
Troast, Robert C., 124–125
Troast Vision & Hearing Center, 124–125
TV. *See* Television
Tylenol, 136
Tyson, Esther, 166

Umbrellas, 137
Unique selling proposition (U.S.P.),
  11–17
  reinventing, 19–26
Uniroyal tires, 3
United Airlines, 199
United Jersey Banks, 69
United Kingdom, 121
United States, 121
Universal aspects to life and marketing,
  189

US magazine, 84
U.S. News & World Report, 4, 166
U.S.P. *See* Unique selling proposition
  (U.S.P.)

Vanderbilt, Mrs. Reginald, 141
Vanity Fair, 211
VCRs, 87
Velcro, 21, 86
Venture capitalists, 71
Victoria's Secret, 129
Video games, 87
Villager's Hardware, 60
Villavicencio, 102
Virgin markets, 32
Visa, 88, 99
Vittel, 190
Vodka, 55, 120, 122
Volkswagen, 3, 40, 79, 98, 132, 206
Volvo, 3, 24, 77, 98, 172, 173, 174, 185
Vuursteen, Karel, 191

Wal-Mart, 47, 53, 58, 59, 100, 122, 123,
  196, 201
Wash & Comb shampoo, 22–23
Water:
  attributes in, 101
  bottled water brands (early 1970s *vs.*
    late 1990s), 6
Waterford crystal, 202
Weatherbeater paint, 196
Web. *See* Internet
WebMD Inc., 134
Welch, Jack, 210
Wellpoint (healthcare), 3
Wells Fargo Bank, 77, 117, 199
Westinghouse, 8
White Castle, 150–151, 185
Whopper. *See* Burger King
Wilkinson, 88
Wingspan.com, 162
Women's hosiery styles (early 1970s *vs.*
  late 1990s), 6

Xerox, 79, 81, 84, 86, 108, 131

Yale, David, 125
Yogurt, 193
Young & Rubicam, 13
Yugo automobile, 121
Yugoslavia, 121

Zagats, 2, 7, 62, 140, 141
Zantac, 158
Zyman, Sergio, 42–43